Hidden Voices

Biblical Women and Our Christian Heritage

Hidden Voices
Biblical Women and Our Christian Heritage

Heidi Bright Parales

SMYTH & HELWYS
PUBLISHING, INC.

Macon, Georgia

ISBN 1-57312-173-8

Hidden Voices
Biblical Women and Our Christian Heritage

Heidi Bright Parales

Smyth & Helwys Publishing, Inc.
6316 Peake Road
Macon, Georgia 31210-3960
1-800-747-3016

Printed in the United States of America.

The paper used in this publication meets the minimum requirements of American Standard for Information Sciences—Permanence of Paper for Printed Library Materials. ANSI Z39.48–1984.

Library of Congress Cataloging-in-Publication Data

Parales, Heidi Bright.
Hidden voices: biblical women and our Christian heritage/ Heidi Bright Parales.
p. cm.
Includes bibliographical references.
ISBN 1-57312-173-8 (alk. paper)
1. Women in the Bible.
2. Women in Christianity.
3. Women—Religious life.
I. Title.
BS575.P26 1998
220.8'3054—dc21 97-50015
CIP

*Chapter 1, "The Eve of Woman," adapted from chapter 4, *God and the Rhetoric of Sexuality* by Phyllis Trible, copyright © 1978 Fortress Press. Used by permission of Augsburg Fortress.

Contents

Introduction

I was so disappointed. With a big sigh, I set aside both the packet of information and my aspirations of working in a church setting. I was a high school student, and had contacted a church to inquire about church-related careers that were available to me. The church gave me a packet containing plenty of information about careers for men in the church, but virtually nothing for women, and certainly nothing at which women could earn a decent living.

Years later, realizing I was not personally suited to the ministry, I decided to attend seminary. I had many questions no one I knew could answer. During my first semester, I walked into a chapel service and, to my surprise, heard a woman preach. She was superb—better than most men I had heard preach. And she was ordained.

Now wait just a minute. Doesn't the Bible say that women are to be silent and submissive in church, not to teach or have authority over men, and that men, as God-ordained heads over women, are to rule over women? How could anyone reconcile these themes with an ordained woman preacher? And why would a God of love bless her with such gifts, and then deny her the use of them in a ministry for which she was so well suited?

Several years later, with surprise and fascination, I discovered there was a woman apostle in the New Testament who was both commended by the apostle Paul and who was imprisoned for her faith. I learned that Phoebe was the deacon and leader of her congregation, and that in the Old Testament, Deborah held the same position of leadership and authority for the Israelites as the judge Samuel.

Perhaps I didn't have enough information, or the right translations or interpretations of the passages about women. So, girding myself with 96 hours of seminary training, including years of language study in Hebrew and Greek, I headed for the local seminary library.

My search for answers spanned about five years and nearly 100 books and articles from several libraries. I found many authors with the same questions who found some intriguing answers. The disharmony of what I had heard before was eventually reconciled during my research. The overarching theme of my study of women in the Bible was that God is not interested in hierarchies, or in male dominance/female submission, or in keeping gifted women out of effective service for the kingdom of heaven.

For example, the Hebrew text in Genesis 1–3 makes it clear that male and female were formed as equals in both creation accounts. The Greek word translated "head," as in 1 Corinthians 11:3, meant "source" in New Testament times. The Ephesian directive for submission includes men submitting to their wives, which is supported by the fact that God specifically told Abraham to submit to Sarah. In addition, one scholar's Greek word studies on 1 Timothy 2:12 provide a completely different, but thoroughly credible, translation of this verse that finally makes real sense.

Overall, modern scholarship reveals that the God in the pages of Scripture is a God who loves femaleness just as much as maleness; a God who creates and loves all human beings equally; and a God who is interested not only in our salvation, but also in human development, human justice, and human equality.

After all, humanity—both male and female—is made in the image of God. How could God love women any less than men? The Hebrew text makes it clear that women were not cursed in Genesis 3:16, despite centuries of interpretations to the contrary. God provided ways for women, as well as men, to serve in effective leadership roles in biblical history and on into the early centuries after Christ. There is no division of ministry mentioned in the Bible; all spiritual gifts are for all Christians, women and men. God is both loving and just in the pages of Scripture, and is no respecter of persons—male or female. Rather, it is humans who sometimes are not interested in justice and equality. It is humans who have created hierarchies, power structures, and systems that sometimes leave others powerless, without voice and hope.

Come explore this issue, with your Bible close at hand and perhaps with a circle of friends. Dive into the difficult passages concerning women—Genesis 2–3; 1 Corinthians 11:3-16, 14:34-36; 1 Peter 3; Ephesians 5; and 1 Timothy 2:11-15. Take another look at how Jesus treated women, including single mothers, women who left their husbands, and destitute widows. Listen to the hidden voices of courageous women who held leadership roles, such as Huldah, the founder of biblical studies; women who led churches in their homes; and Priscilla, who taught Apollos, a man whom Paul considered his equal. Consider what it means to have a relationship of mutuality and equality with others, including spouses. Finally, find out for yourself about the feminine images of God in the Bible, such as when God is described as conceiving, giving birth, and gathering together like a mother hen.

Each chapter opens with an anecdote about a woman and then proceeds with a discussion of issues that leads to greater understanding of what equality and mutuality should mean in Christian churches. Each chapter is followed by provocative discussion questions that address both the biblical content of the passages and how they relate to everyday life.

Discover the true heritage of all Christian women and what it means to have real freedom in Christ. You just might find yourself amazed, inspired, and motivated to greater depths in your walk with God. You also might find ways to bring others into dialogue with you about this important issue, thereby enriching and broadening their relationships with each other and with God.

Chapter 1

The Eve of Woman

Genesis 1–3

Eufame Macalyane was burned alive in 1591 for seeking pain relief when she gave birth to her two sons. The rationale behind the decision to burn Macalyane, a Scottish woman of rank, was that God had cursed women with pain in childbirth. To prevent her from experiencing pain during labor would be a circumvention of God's will.

In 1847, Sir James Y. Simpson, a Scottish physician and surgeon, was able to convince the medical community that God would not be opposed to his use of chloroform to anesthetize women during childbirth. His argument? God used anesthesia when performing divine surgery on Adam in Genesis 2:21.[1]

Eufame Macalyane suffered an agonizing death because of a false assumption about the biblical creation accounts. At least a dozen other false assumptions have arisen from English interpretations of the creation account in Genesis 2–3. Among them are: males are superior to females, woman was created to help man, and woman was responsible for sin and the fall of humanity. Theologian John Calvin added to the problems this text created for women when he wrote in the sixteenth century that God commanded men to rule women and assigned women the role of obedience to men.[2] The passage has even been used as justification for battering and abusing women.

Women have accepted these translations because they have had little choice. Throughout history, very few women have been fortunate enough to learn how to read and to receive any kind of substantive education. Only during the past few decades have women had the opportunity to attend seminary and learn the original languages of Hebrew and Greek. Prepared with solid educations, these women have taken a fresh look at the worn-out interpretations of biblical passages concerning women. As a result, they have begun to call into question many of the assumptions people have brought to the

Bible for thousands of years. Fortunately for women, they have discovered that the Hebrew text of the Old Testament never supports these negative assumptions.

Creation of *Ha-adam* and the Woman

The negative assumptions begin with the second creation account in Genesis 2. The creation of the earth and humanity are closely linked in this chapter. God forms "the earth," *ha-adamah,* in Genesis 2:4. The Hebrew word *ha-adamah* consists of a definite article *ha,* translated "the," and the noun *adamah,* translated "earth." *Adamah* here is a word with a feminine ending, indicated by the letters "ah" at the end of the word. Although in the Hebrew language nouns have masculine and feminine endings, this does not mean the object is sexually masculine or feminine. The earth, *adamah,* has a feminine ending, but the earth is not sexually feminine.

So God creates the earth, but has no one to take care of it. In verse 7, when God begins the process of creating humanity to cultivate the earth, God forms *ha-adam.* The word *ha-adam* carries much significance in the unfolding narrative. The Hebrew text literally says God formed *ha-adam,* "the earth being," from *ha-adamah,* "the earth." The writer is using a play on words to show the similarity between the earth and the earth being.[3] The play on these Hebrew words, used to create a point, is made obvious to the Hebrew reader by the writer's repeated use of the nouns *adamah* and *adam.* The word *adam* occurs twenty-nine times, and the word *adamah* appears sixteen times in the first five chapters of Genesis.

In Genesis 2:4-17, *ha-adam* is given a grammatically masculine gender, but not specifically a masculine sexuality. Instead, *adam* is used in a generic sense, as indicated by the definite article *ha,* "the," before the noun *adam.*[4] It is not until much later in the story that Adam is used as a formal name for a sexual male human being. If one were to find an English equivalent for a generic *ha-adam* and a related proper name, Adam, one might find a similar word situation in the generic phrase "the buddy" for any person, versus the formal name "Buddy" for a male.

Again, there is no indication in the Hebrew text that *ha-adam* is biologically male. *Ha-adam* is not described as a man or as a woman, nor as a combination of both. In fact, *ha-adam* is given no gender identity. It is too early in the story for this information, especially because God is not yet finished with the creation process. Therefore, the assertion that the male figure formally named Adam was the first human being on the earth is a big assumption.[5] Specific gender identity for males and females comes in Genesis 2:18-24, after God performs "surgery" on the earth being.

After the creation of *ha-adam,* God places the earth being in the Garden of Eden and tells it to cultivate the garden and to eat from every tree except the tree of knowledge of good and evil. The earth being remains the only one of its kind—a separate creation from the animals and birds, a distinct being standing alone and unique.

Apparently, God realizes the earth being is lonely because there is no one similar with whom *ha-adam* can form a relationship. So, in verse 18, God makes a promise to the earth being; *ha-adam* will no longer be alone. God will create a suitable (*knegdwo*) companion (*ezer*). In Hebrew, the word *ezer* was often translated "helper," which has been used for millennia to imply that this new creature would be an assistant only, one in an inferior position to *ha-adam* because it would be created for *ha-adam* and after *ha-adam.*[6]

This assumption has no basis in the story. The word *ezer* is used more than a dozen times in the Old Testament in reference to God (see Ps 121:1-2). God would hardly be considered inferior to or an assistant to *ha-adam.* Actually, because it is used in reference to God, it is possible *ezer* could refer to one in a superior position. The Hebrew text in verse 18, however, does not support this conclusion. The woman is not superior to *ha-adam* because she is created to be a companion. Rather, in this verse, *ezer* is combined with the word *knegdwo,* translated here as the phrase, "suitable for him."

The Hebrew language often combines several words into one word. In this case, the root word for *knegdwo* is *neged. Neged* literally refers to something in front of or in the presence of another. The root word *neged,* when used as a noun, refers to rulers and leaders in the Old Testament. The word in Genesis, however, is altered by the prefix "k," which refers to some type of similarity or comparison. So the word appears to refer to someone similar to, yet in front of, *ha-adam,* almost as if the earth being is looking into a mirror image of itself.

This phrase indicates that God intends to fashion another creature who will not be inferior or superior to *ha-adam,* but rather one with whom *ha-adam* can share a relationship of total equality. The two will become suitable companions, which will relieve *ha-adam*'s aloneness.[7]

But God takes some time to get to the climactic event that brings about the height of creation. First, God forms the animals and brings them to *ha-adam* so the earth being can give them names. Here, *ha-adam* does as requested, "calling . . . the name" of each creature, and thereby exercising power over them. The animals are thereby subordinated to the earth being.[8]

Finally, in verse 21, God begins to fulfill the promise for companionship:[9] God places *ha-adam* in a sleep and removes one of the earth being's ribs (*sela*). Then God builds the rib into woman (*ishshah*) and brings her to *ha-adam.* God seems to be using an anesthetic for the "surgery" on the earth being.

Verse 21 became the key in the struggle by Dr. James Y. Simpson when he sought, in 1847, to use chloroform to help women through childbirth. He saw the pain of childbirth as unnecessary, given the medical practices of his day. His opponents disagreed, denouncing his activities as a circumvention of God's "curse" on women. Simpson was not to be so easily stopped. He came back with the argument that God used anesthesia on "Adam" for the first recorded surgery. His supposed logic eventually won the day, and women were soon allowed medical intervention for the pain of labor and delivery.

The divine surgery Simpson referred to involved the removal of a rib, or *sela*, from *ha-adam. Sela* can indicate more than a single bone; it can be translated as the earth being's side.[10] The woman is derived from the creature's side, which symbolically indicates her equality with *ha-adam.* If she had been taken from the earth being's head, this would imply her superiority; if from *ha-adam*'s feet, it would imply her inferiority.

There is no indication of inequality, either, in the substance from which the woman is formed. God uses dust or ground, which is material from the earth, to create the earth being (Gen 2:7), yet the earth being is never considered subordinate to the earth. So, in verse 22, the Creator takes raw material from the earth being and personally fashions a female and brings her to the earth being, yet she is not considered subordinate to the earth being.[11] Every creature thus far, including *ha-adam*, is created from the ground. The woman, however, is unique because she is the only creature formed from living flesh.[12]

After fashioning the woman, God brings her to *ha-adam.* In verse 23, the effects of the surgery on *ha-adam* are clarified. *Ha-adam* says, "This at last is bone of my bones and flesh of my flesh; this one shall be called Woman *(ishshah)*, for out of Man *(ish)* this one was taken." Here, the Hebrew switches to completely new nouns to describe the two beings. This change indicates an alteration in who they have become, both individually and as a couple. *Ha-adam* moves into a new personal awareness, calling himself *ish*, or male, and the woman *ishshah*, or female. Here again the narrator uses a play on words. The man gives himself a new identity with the word *ish*, thereby revealing that he has acknowledged a change in himself. No longer is he the earth being. From this point forward, he knows he is male, and so identifies himself with the term *ish*. His transformation seems to have occurred with the removal of the *sela* from *ha-adam*'s side.[13] He also uses a play on words to indicate his similarity to the woman by taking the word he uses for himself and adding a feminine ending to it to identify the female. In this case, the feminine ending indicates more than grammar; it reveals sexuality because the word itself means "female."[14]

By using *ish* and *ishshah*, the male demonstrates his recognition of their biological differences and also realizes that he has himself been changed into a sexual being. Although he has changed, he is still referred to as *ha-adam*. This reference indicates that he has some connection with the earth being who existed before surgery. Now, however, *ha-adam* refers to a biological male, not to an earth being with no sexual identification.[15] Through *ha-adam*'s delighted exclamation, he places emphasis on the similarity between himself and the woman, while also recognizing that each one's gender identity is dependent on the other's gender.[16]

As *ish* celebrates their similarity, he never gives any hint of being in a superior role to the female. Although he does call her *ishshah*, he does not formally name her as he had the animals earlier in the story. With the animals, *ha-adam* used a naming formula. He "called the name" of the animals, thereby establishing power over them. With the female, however, he only "calls" her, not actually naming her. He simply identifies with her. In fact, he does not come up with the term; God has already called her *ishshah* in verse 22.[17] Both the male and the female remain nameless at this point in the story. Adam is still not the male's formal name. In this part of the story, he is still referred to as *ha-adam*, "the adam"—sort of like "the buddy" or "the guy."

Along with recognizing their gender differences, the male realizes that the woman has been made of the same substance as himself, so his joy focuses on their relatedness, their similarity. Their alikeness is further emphasized by *ha-adam*'s words in verse 24: "Therefore a man (*ish*) leaves his father and his mother and clings to his wife (*ishshah*), and they become one flesh."

Ha-adam differentiates between his maleness and her femaleness in verse 23, but now he brings the two of them together to form one flesh. They are of the same substance, the same bone, the same flesh. *Ha-adam* is no longer alone in the garden.

To emphasize their oneness, *ha-adam* uses the verb "to cleave," a Hebrew word that indicates strong personal attachment to another. By cleaving, the two become one bone, one flesh. By becoming one flesh, they share a relationship based on equality. When the two become one, there is no superiority of one over another nor submission of one to another. They do not own or control each other. Instead, they become a part of each other.

In verse 24, it appears that the man is the one who leaves his family of origin to create a new union with his wife. The man is identified by his parents, whom he leaves. The woman, however, is not identified by any other person. Rather, the woman appears to be without family, without ties; she is a free agent.[18] Although this passage was probably written during the period of King David's reign, it stands in stark contrast to the accepted practices of that time. In a patrilinial society, the woman leaves her family of origin—in which she is considered the property of the head of her household—and goes to live with her husband to become his property. This verse, however, may be the remnant of a different type of society, a society in which the male leaves his family of origin and goes to live with the woman and her family of origin. Such a society is considered matrilocal, because the males go to live with their wives' families.

Nowhere in this creation account is there any hint that woman is created to be man's housekeeper, cook, or the bearer of his children. Procreation is never mentioned, nor are these other tasks. The male and the female are created to be equal partners in life.

The story line continues with a new use of the term *ha-adam* emerging. In verse 25, the male is referred to as *ha-adam*, showing that he has a historical relation to the earth being, but now has a new biological identity in relation to the female. When the text refers to *ha-adam* and his wife, the possessive form "his" refers not to his owning his wife but to the woman who is a part of him, who is bone of his bone and flesh of his flesh.[19]

Ha-adam as Male and Female

The term *ha-adam* has a similar meaning in another creation account in Genesis.

> Let us make humankind (*ha-adam*) in our image, according to our likeness; and let them have dominion over the fish of the sea, and over the birds of the air, and over the cattle, over all the wild animals of the earth, and over every creeping thing that creeps upon the earth. (1:26)

In this verse, *ha-adam* refers to "them" who are to rule over the earth and all its creatures. *Ha-adam* cannot possibly be just the first male in this verse; "them" is a term that includes more than one person. Who those people are is clarified somewhat in the next verse: "So God created humankind (*ha-adam*) in his image, in the image of God he created them; male and female he created them."

This verse, then, provides the answer: "The adam," initially referred to as "him," is quickly referred to as "them"; and "them" in this verse is defined as "male and female." This shows some parallels with the creation account in Genesis 2, in which *ha-adam*, the single earth being, becomes male and female.

Because *ha-adam* is a singular word in this passage that represents both male and female, the word can be translated "human" or "humanity." Humanity encompasses both male and female. Yet, humanity is referred to with the singular "him." This appears to indicate that male and female together form a oneness, a single unit that works together. There is no separation, no hierarchy, no competition within this unity. God sees *ha-adam* as part of creation and calls it "very good."

In addition, *ha-adam* is created as a reflection of God. Because both male and female are embodied in *ha-adam*, it takes both a male and a female to form a reflection or image of God. Male alone or female alone cannot properly reflect the image of God; something will always be missing. Both together give one a better understanding of God's nature.

This identification of gender for the male and the female is only given to the humans, not to the animals. So here, to be male and female as human sexual beings is to refer to God, not to biological reproduction. Here, God is referred to as Elohim in the text. Elohim is a plural noun, so it can literally refer to more than one god. This is especially the case when Elohim refers to God's self as "we." Because God is referred to as Elohim in the first creation account, the text is considered part of the Priestly version of the Old Testament. The Priestly version refers to parts of the Old Testament that show concern for the priestly office that was developed later by the Hebrews.

In this Priestly account, Elohim does not refer to a singular being any more than *ha-adam* refers to the first male. There seems to be a mirror effect here in that humans, made up of male and female, give a dim reflection of Elohim, who is made up of the Creator, Redeemer, and Holy Spirit. This concept allows for unity, equality, and complementariness both among the aspects of God and between male and female. One thing in this verse is certain: *ha-adam* is not a male. It is only later, in chapter 4, that Adam becomes a proper name used in reference to the father of humankind.

To both the male and the female, God gives the following command: "Be fruitful and multiply, and fill the earth and subdue it; and have dominion over the fish of the sea and over the birds of the air and over every living thing that moves upon the earth." In the Hebrew, the commands are given in plural form. Both man and woman are given the directive to be fruitful and multiply, to subdue the earth, and to have dominion over the creatures. Therefore, if male and female do not rule jointly, they disobey God's explicit command. There also is no differentiation between sexes when it comes to tasks they are to perform or roles they are to take. Both are granted equal authority, equal responsibility, and equal work.

The command implies a hierarchy of order. The male and the female together, as a single unit, are to rule the earth and the other living creatures. For the relationship between the female and the male, no chain of command is given. Both are given equal stature, authority, and command to subdue the earth. No human is given the right to lord it over another human. Humans are given their work to do together as equals.

The Fall

What happened to this God-designated equality? The answer is provided in chapter 3, where the story of *ha-adam* progresses into what has come to be known as the fall of humanity. The serpent who enters the scene here is described as one of the wild beasts created by God, one over whom *ha-adam* is called to exercise dominion. Nowhere is the serpent described as a demon or as the devil.

This serpent is no ordinary creature, though. It is described as "the craftiest of all the wild beasts," and it proceeds to exercise its cunning against the earthly couple. It chooses to address the woman rather than the man, asking her if God really does not allow them to eat from every tree. Because the man and the woman are one flesh, the serpent probably knows it can ensnare them both by addressing one of them. It asks her the question, but twists the words God has earlier commanded: "Did God say, 'You (plural) shall not eat from any tree in the garden'?" In reply, the woman repeats more accurately what God has commanded. Not only does she know about the prohibition, which is addressed to *ha-adam* in the beginning of the story, but she also owns it for herself. When she repeats the prohibition, she quotes God, saying, "You (plural) shall not eat of . . . it."

In Genesis 2:16-17, God addresses the words of prohibition about the fruit of the tree to *ha-adam*, yet here the woman assumes responsibility for them. There is no indication that the man tells the woman about the prohibition. It is more likely, based on the contents of the story, that the woman is part of *ha-adam* in the beginning of the story, before being separated out.

When the woman replies to the serpent, she not only repeats God's prohibition, but adds to it the idea that she cannot even touch the fruit. Here, she reveals that she is thinking beyond the mere command to its implications, revealing her reasoning ability and her self-discipline.[20] She resists the temptation of the serpent.

The serpent is not so easily deterred, though. It responds by challenging the woman, telling her she will not die, but will become like God if she eats the fruit. The woman listens to the serpent and begins to think beyond the simple prohibition God gave them. The tree begins to represent something she wants very badly—knowledge. The rest of the garden will no longer satisfy her need to know.[21]

She decides to act on her own initiative. She doesn't discuss the situation with the man, who is with her, but openly reaches out and eats the food. She also gives some to the man. The man, who has stood by throughout the conversation, yet who has said and done nothing, willingly chooses for himself and decides to eat the fruit. During the entire scene, he quietly stands nearby and never once breathes a word of resistance to the idea of eating the fruit.

Both the female and the male are tempted. Neither tempts the other; the woman is not the temptress here. Both fall victim to the temptation. Neither proves to be more righteous or obedient than the other.

The narrator of the story then begins to tell the consequences of their disobedience. Their eyes are opened, they realize they are naked, and they make clothing to cover their sudden revelation concerning their sexuality.

Now they feel shame. They hide, but God comes, seeking the man and asking him some questions. The man replies that he hid because he was naked and afraid. When God asks him why he knows he is naked, the man takes on the role of the victim and begins by blaming others. First, he tells God about the woman's activity, though without saying she tempted him. Then he places part of the responsibility for the situation on God for giving him the woman. Only after playing the victim does he reveal his own role in their plight—he ate of the fruit. Sin enters in as he finds it difficult to take responsibility for his own action.[22]

After listening, God asks the woman what she has done. The woman, in turn, also plays the victim when she blames the serpent. Yet she, too, eventually accepts responsibility for her actions—she ate of the fruit. Her reluctance to take responsibility for her actions also is evident.[23]

Gone is the idyllic union of the first couple. Gone is the mutuality, the equality, the delight in the one flesh they represent. Gone is what God calls "very good" in the first creation account.[24] In its place, the man and the woman feel enmity toward each other. Their relationship to each other has broken down, and so has their relationship with God. Sin ripens and takes hold, and its consequences are announced by God.

God's Response

God begins by judging the three beings, as a human judge would do in a court of law. The two humans have confessed their guilt, and God now gives a ruling. God does not, however, mete out punishment; that will come later.[25] For now, God starts with the serpent, telling it,

> Because you have done this, cursed are you among all animals and among all wild creatures; upon your belly you shall go, and dust you shall eat all the days of your life. I will put enmity between you and the woman, and between your offspring and hers; he will strike your head, and you will strike his heel. (vv. 14-15)

In these two verses, God directly curses the serpent where the text reads, "cursed are you." The serpent is the only one of the threesome that is actually cursed.

The woman is not cursed by God. She is addressed in verse 16: "To the woman (*ishshah*) he said, 'I will greatly increase your pangs (*issabon*) in childbearing; in pain (*issabon*) you shall bring forth children.' " No cursing language is used in this verse. God does not issue the command, "You must experience great pain in childbirth." Rather, the simple future tense form of the verb is used to describe what will happen to the woman, not what must be. She must pay the consequences of her actions; she brought the pain upon herself. There is no prescription for pain in childbirth, only a description of the consequences of her actions.[26]

Further consequences are described in the second half of verse 16: "Your desire (*teshuqa*) shall be for your husband (*ish*), and he shall rule over you." Take a closer look at the word *teshuqa,* which is commonly translated "desire." With such a translation, the desire the woman experiences could simply be a longing to return to the idyllic state she existed in before she ate the fruit—when she and *ish* were bone of bone and flesh of flesh. She has experienced the joy of equality and mutuality with the man.[27] Her desire is certainly understandable, especially considering the consequences of the judgment on her relationship with the man.

There is another valid English word for *teshuqa.* In several ancient manuscripts, *teshuqa* is translated "to turn." With such a translation, the phrase reads, "Yet you turn to your husband, and he would rule over you." Here, *teshuqa* can refer to when a woman turns to her husband for her needs and does not turn to God for them. If a wife looks to her husband for everything, rather than to God, then she places tremendous power in her husband's hands, which he can easily use to rule over her. This leaves the choice of who rules the woman in her own hands.

Notice next that the husband also has a choice in the matter. While the woman desires either mutuality with the man or looks to him instead of to God, the man's desire is to rule the woman. He wants to set up a hierarchy in which he dominates the woman. When the Hebrew text says, "he would rule over you," it uses a simple future tense form of the verb "to rule." In Semitic languages, there is no sense of obligation in the future tense of verbs; man is not required to rule woman. The man has the option of ruling the woman, if the woman turns to him. Once again, in this passage, God is describing the future, not ordering or prescribing it.[28]

The relationship between man and woman is dramatically changed for the worse. The joy, harmony, and mutuality of life in Eden has vaporized. Now, dominated by the man, the woman's role in the story becomes subordinated to the role of *ha-adam.*

God tells the man the results of his sin in verses 17-19:

> And to the man he said, "Because you have listened to the voice of your wife (*ishshah*), and have eaten of the tree about which I commanded you, (saying), 'You shall not eat of it,' cursed is the ground because of you; in toil (*issabon*) you shall eat of it all the days of your life; thorns and thistles it shall bring forth for you; and you shall eat the plants of the field. By the sweat of your face you shall eat bread until you return to the ground, for out of it you were taken; you are dust, and to dust you shall return."

Again, God does not curse the man; God merely describes the consequences of his actions, using a simple future tense form of the verb. Rather, it is the earth—*ha-adamah*—that is cursed.[29]

This curse does affect *ha-adam*, as his cultivation of the ground, which God created to be easy, has became hard labor. The word for his hard labor (*issabon*) is the same word used to describe the woman's labor.[30] The judgment on the male and the female is equivalent, showing that both are equally responsible for their individual choices, and both will pay dearly for their actions. Both are treated equally by God; God shows no preferential treatment to the male.

In Genesis 2:15, God asks *ha-adam*, the earth being, to cultivate the earth. In Genesis 1:28, God asks both the female and the male to be fruitful and multiply. Both the male and the female are told to fulfill both commands. Now these activities have simply become much more difficult. Hard labor is the result of sin for both the man and the woman. If one insists that women must experience pain in childbirth and must let their husbands rule them, then men must also be forced to do manual labor in the fields, battling thorns and thistles, to fulfill their part of the consequences for the sin of the man.

After announcing the consequences for their actions, the narrator stops using the word *ish*, or male. In its place, *ha-adam* is used for the remainder of the story.[31] Here, *ha-adam* takes on yet a third meaning in the second creation account. *Ha-adam,* the original earth creature from Genesis 2:4-17, became identified as male after the woman was created. After the fall, *ha-adam* changes again and signifies something new in the story.

In verse 20, *ha-adam* begins to exercise power over the woman by using the naming formula on her: "The man named his wife Eve." Earlier in the story, the earth being called the names of the animals, exercising dominion over them. Now he "calls the name" of the woman Eve, following the same pattern he used on the animals. He asserts his dominance over the woman, not as a divine right but as one ruling over the companion who was created as an equal for him.[32]

After the man's overtly domineering act, God steps in to clothe them both.

> Then the Lord God said, "See, the man (*ha-adam*) has become like one of us, knowing good and evil; and now, he might reach out his hand and take also from the tree of life, and eat, and live forever."—therefore the Lord God sent him forth from the Garden of Eden, to till the ground (*ha-adamah*) from which he was taken. He drove out the man (*ha-adam*); and at the east of the Garden of Eden he placed the cherubim, and a sword flaming and turning to guard the way to the tree of life. (vv. 22-24)

Finally, God explains the need for punishment beyond the judgment—so the humans, with the knowledge of good and evil, will not live forever. The possibility of death, as God promised in 2:17, has become reality. The two humans have to be removed from the garden.

The text here says only *ha-adam* is like "one of us" and is expelled from the garden. The woman is not even mentioned in these two verses. We know she was expelled as well, because in the following chapter the couple has children. So what becomes of her? Why does she become invisible in this passage?

Perhaps the narrator of the story reverts to a generic term for the couple, a masculine form that makes the woman invisible but leaves the man still visible and appearing as the primary individual. This would fit in well with verse 16, in which the woman turns to her husband and he will rule over her.[33] Not only has *ha-adam* begun his rule over the woman, but the woman has became invisible—voiceless, unseen, unheard, devalued.

The antagonism between the sexes has begun, not by God's design or command but by the fact that men and women have became unequal in each other's eyes. The consequences of their actions leave the woman vulnerable to becoming subservient and subordinate to the male. The conflict between the sexes extends to the created world as well, since now the earth itself is cursed.

The beauty of sexual balance, equality, and differentiation has turned into the ugliness of sexism. Yet this sexism seems to end as soon as the twosome settle in their new home. Ironically, Adam does no more speaking after leaving the Garden of Eden. Rather, Eve, who becomes invisible in chapter 3, displays power in chapter 4. In 4:1, she proclaims her creative powers when she conceives and gives birth to Cain. Because she is the one speaking in the text, she probably is the one who names her first two sons, because in verse 25, she is specifically shown to name her third son Seth. Adam is strangely quiet; he certainly is not shown controlling or dominating Eve in any way. Perhaps the couple is able to return, in some way, to the harmony, equality, and mutuality they experienced before they ate of the tree in the middle of the Garden of Eden.

Questions for Reflection

1. What does it mean to you to be made in the image of God?
2. In the woman's conversation with the serpent, what positive qualities do you see in her?
3. When their eyes were opened, what did the man and the woman experience?

4. How proper is it to continue to blame Eve for the fall of humanity? How does this tendency to blame compare to what the male did in Genesis 3:12?
5. If you have experienced the labor and delivery of a child, did you feel cursed by God? How do you feel about it now?
6. If you are a woman in a serious relationship with a man, do you find it easier to turn to him than to God to meet your needs? In what cases is it appropriate for a woman to turn to a man? When is it inappropriate? How does this relate to Acts 5:29?
7. If you are a woman, do you sometimes feel invisible in a man's world? If you are a man, do you also find this to be true? If so, what concrete things can be done to counteract this feeling?
8. In what ways have you experienced sexism in your life? What can be done to counteract it in a positive way?
9. In what ways can you make your relationships with the opposite sex more equal and mutual?
10. What can women do to regain value in the eyes of society?
11. In what ways can the mutuality and equality of the Garden of Eden be restored in your life?
12. The text says the earth was cursed because of human sin. The earth need not necessarily be cursed by our behavior, yet land is raped and the planet is heading toward destruction. What can we do to prevent this destruction from continuing?
13. In what ways have traditional interpretations of the second creation story affected your view of women? Has this view changed?

Notes

[1]Andrew Dickson White, *A History of the Warfare of Science with Theology* (New York: D. Appleton and Co., 1925) 2:62-63.

[2]Rosemary Radford Ruether, *Sexism and God-Talk* (Boston: Beacon Press, 1983) 98.

[3]Phyllis Trible, *God and the Rhetoric of Sexuality* (Philadelphia: Fortress Press, 1978) 79.

[4]Ibid., 80.

[5]Ibid.

[6]Ibid., 90.

[7]David Freeman also makes an excellent case for translating the phrase *ezer knegdwo* as "power equal to," referring to the newly created woman and her relationship to *ha-adam.* See David Freeman, "Woman a Power Equal to

Man: Translation of Woman as a 'Fit Helpmeet' for Man Is Questioned," *Biblical Archaeology Review* 9, no. 1 (January/February 1983): 56-58.

[8]Trible, 92.

[9]Perhaps God waits to create *ha-adam*'s other until *ha-adam* names the animals, because then *ha-adam* could recognize its loneliness. See Avivah Gottlieb Zornberg, *The Beginning of Desire* (New York: Doubleday, 1995) 15-16.

[10]Koehler-Baumgartner, *Lexicon in Veteris Testamenti Libros* (Leiden: E. J. Brill, 1958) 805.

[11]Trible, 101.

[12]Ibid., 96.

[13]Ibid., 98.

[14]Ibid.

[15]Ibid.

[16]Ibid., 98, 99.

[17]Ibid., 99, 100.

[18]Ibid., 104.

[19]Carol Meyers, *Discovering Eve* (New York: Oxford University Press, 1988) 110.

[20]Trible, 110.

[21]Ibid., 112-13.

[22]Ibid., 119.

[23]Ibid., 120.

[24]Ibid.

[25]Ibid., 123.

[26]Mary Hayter, *The New Eve in Christ* (Grand Rapids: Wm. B. Eerdmans Publishing Co., 1987) 114.

[27]Trible, 128.

[28]Ibid.

[29]Ibid., 130.

[30]Ibid., 127.

[31]Ibid., 133.

[32]Ibid.

[33]Ibid., 135.

Chapter 2

Women Leaders in the Old Testament

The very stones cry out that at least a handful of women held important leadership roles between 27 B.C.E. and the sixth century, according to research conducted by Bernadette Brooten, a professor at Harvard Divinity School. These women's titles ranged from elder to president to priestess [(h)ierissa] *of the synagogue. The woman's name Gael is inscribed on a stone in Asia Minor, proclaiming her the patron or presiding officer of a Jewish congregation. Men's names are listed below hers. Another leader was Rufina, proclaimed as president of her synagogue* [archisynagogos] *on her tomb inscription. As president, her responsibilities would have included overseeing services, preaching, and teaching.*[1] *Sophia of Gortyn was elder and head of the synagogue of Kisamos, according to an inscription made in the fourth or fifth century. These are just three of nineteen women whose names are written in stone, testifying to some of the important leadership roles Jewish women held.*[2]

Handwritten accounts tell of another woman leader during the second century C.E. The Jewish woman Beruria, who demonstrated considerable spiritual and intellectual gifts, was renowned for centuries for her prowess with the Torah. She set high standards for studying the Torah as a rabbinical student. Her comments on the Torah were turned into Jewish rabbinical law. In addition, she became a master teacher of the Torah and lived a highly moral life. She exceeded all the requirements for becoming a rabbi, although she was never actually referred to as a rabbi in the texts that have survived.[3]

Like Beruria, handwritten accounts tell of numerous other women leaders, especially in the Old Testament. Their memories are preserved for us, even if in abbreviated form, in the pages of Israelite history. In early Israel, before the onset of the monarchy, women held an important cultural role in society. During this time, the household was the primary unit of society and therefore the location of cultural power. These households consisted of large, complex, multigenerational family units that were isolated in pockets of the highlands west of the Jordan River, for example, Galilee, Samaria, and Judea.

Here, life was extremely difficult. Disease took a heavy toll on family groups (see Num 26:1-2).[4] Water was usually in short supply, the terrain was hilly, and the soil quality was poor.[5] The early Israelites were probably pioneer farmers in this area, turning the forested hills into farmland (Josh 17:18). It was probably the men who dug cisterns and cleared the land, while the women worked to provide a ready food supply.[6] The farmers terraced the hillsides to improve crop production, but a huge investment in labor was required to create and maintain them.[7] This meant all individuals in a family group were interdependent on each other for survival. Everything the group needed had to be produced by the group. Therefore, early Israelite women played an extremely important role in the family unit. Not only was the demand for their physical labor heightened, but the demand for more labor in the form of children made their reproductive role critical to group survival.[8]

Women probably performed tasks requiring technical skill, such as making pottery and weaving, because their roles were probably somewhat restricted by their care of children. The women probably were in charge of the extremely time-consuming and difficult job of turning raw materials into edible food. This gave them the authority to say how the food would be used by group members, which meant they had control over a large portion of the family unit's economic resources.[9]

Women also held status in the household in the area of parental authority. Children, probably adult members of a multigenerational household unit, were told to honor both their mother and their father (Exod 20:12). In Exodus 21:15, a sentence of death was passed on a child who struck either the mother or father. (The harshness of the sentence mentioned here was probably due to the extreme need among family members to cooperate just to survive). In contrast, Hammurabi's code no. 195, written in the eighteenth century B.C.E., addressed what to do if a child struck his father; the mother was not included.[10] So in early Israelite society, the authority of the mother over the children, including adult children, probably matched that of the father.

Another factor affecting the status of women in early Israel was the lack of a public sphere of life. There were no central political organizations or large-scale public works. All labor remained within the family unit, giving women control over much of it.

Based on anthropological and archaeological evidence, early Israelite society was highly agrarian, with women and men greatly interdependent upon each other for survival. In such gender-balanced societies, women contributed about 40 percent to the household economy, despite the fact women spent much of their teenage and adult years bearing and caring for children.[11] Anthropologists have found that when the ratio of women's work is 40 percent and the men's 60 percent, women tend to reach a high level of status and prestige in that society.[12] In Leviticus 27:7, a valuation of 40 percent is given to women over age 60, revealing the high status of women in premonarchic Israel. While men held recognized positions of leadership or authority, the women probably held a great deal of power themselves through their ability to control important aspects of family life.[13] Their status within the household unit may even have been more powerful than that of the men.[14]

During this time period, some Hebrew women's leadership abilities extended beyond the household unit. Their authority was closely patterned after the leadership positions held by men. The woman Sheerah, for example, had three cities built under her direction (1 Chron 7:24). Women also were judges and prophets during that time period. They were not permitted to be priests, however. There are perhaps two reasons for this.

First, the ancients believed that one's soul resided in one's blood (Lev 17:10-14). The shedding of blood was believed to be a violation of God's command. Therefore, a woman menstruating was considered impure or unclean. A woman who was unclean could not come before Yahweh as a representative of the people.[15] This taboo would have severely limited the role of women in the priesthood.

Second, the Israelites were surrounded by other religious groups that practiced what was called sacred prostitution, consisting of sexual practices in the sanctuary done as fertility rites. Perhaps the greatest problems for the Hebrews were created by the worship of the fertility-goddess Asherah. Goddess rituals often included intercourse with temple prostitutes, male or female. This became of greatest concern during the time of the monarchs. The Israelites wanted nothing to do with this practice, so they probably restricted the priesthood to one gender. Because of the blood taboo, males were the logical choice for members of the priesthood. Not just any male could become a priest, however. He had to be a member of the Levite clan and from the house of Aaron, and have no physical defect (Lev 21:17-23).

God's use of priests was a concession to the Israelites. When the people were ready, God provided a way for all humans to become part of the royal priesthood, with Christ as the high priest. In the meantime, women were not permitted into the priesthood. Yet this did not affect their status in the eyes of their society. Early Israelites generally did not consider women inferior or oppress them. Rather, Israelite society allowed them to follow the call of God in other ways.

Those early women who followed the call of God and carried a lot of authority included women mentioned in the Torah, several prophets and wise women, and a woman who was both a judge and a military leader.

Women of the Torah

Sarah was just as important in establishing the covenant line as Abraham was. Her name was changed, just as was Abraham's name. She was told she would become the mother of nations (Gen 17:16). God did not use Ishmael, son of Abraham and Hagar, as inheritor of the covenant, even though Ishmael was the firstborn of Abraham. Instead, God chose the son of Sarah and Abraham. The Israelites became the daughters and sons of Sarah as well as of Abraham. Also, only the children of Sarah were buried with her and Abraham at Mamre.

Sarah held great authority within her family unit. In fact, her authority was great enough that at one point God commanded Abraham to obey her (Gen 21:12). Sarah wanted Ishmael, Abraham's son with Hagar, to leave so Isaac would be the primary son. Abraham went to God in his distress, yet God commanded Abraham to submit to Sarah's authority. He obeyed God and followed Sarah's wish, expelling Ishmael. Sarah demonstrated that she was no inferior, submissive female. She had a strong personality, and she exercised it as a partner to Abraham. God upheld and affirmed her in this role as partner.

Sarah's maid, Hagar, may not have been chosen as the mother of Israel, but she stands out as a unique figure in the Old Testament for her boldness with God. She is the only person in the Old Testament who "called the name" (*qr' sm*) of Yahweh, using a naming formula (Gen 16:13a). In all other passages, individuals such as Abraham "called *upon* the name" (*qr' bsm*) of Yahweh, using a term for invocation rather than directly naming God (see Gen 12:8; 13:4). In addition, Hagar was the first in all of Scripture to receive a divine visitation (Gen 16:7). The angel of the Lord told her to return to the tents of Sarah, probably because Hagar would need assistance in giving birth and raising her child. This also would establish Ishmael as Abraham's firstborn child (see Deut 21:15-17).[16]

Although Hagar and her son Ishmael were disinherited by Abraham and Sarah, some women in ancient Israel found ways to protect their inheritance. Rachel, Jacob's second wife, was one such woman. There is evidence in the Old Testament of matrilocality, when a man leaves his family of origin to live with his wife's family. Jacob practiced it when he left his father's house and went to live with his mother's brother, Laban. He stayed for twenty years and married Laban's two daughters, Leah and Rachel. Jacob broke with custom when he left his wife's locality and moved with his family and belongings back to his father's locality.

Among those belongings were Laban's teraphim. Teraphim were sacred idols the youngest daughter was responsible for. The teraphim gave the daughter the responsibility for the family's religious obligations.[17] According to Nuzi documents that include information about social customs of the people of Haran, where Rachel lived, possession of the teraphim also symbolized one's title to an inheritance.[18] When Rachel left with the teraphim, she was laying claim to her inheritance. Similarly, Rachel's sister Leah laid claim to her right to name her own children, something that later would be denied to women (see Luke 1:57-66).

Several generations later, the Israelites living in Egypt would not have inherited the Promised Land without the wisdom and pluck of a handful of Hebrew women. These women defied the commands of men, making the great exodus from Egypt possible. They had the support and sanction of God in creatively and peacefully usurping the domination of men.

First, there were the midwives, Shiphrah and Puah, who could not bring themselves to kill the Hebrew male infants, but sagely found a way to avoid bringing disaster on their own heads for it (Exod 2). As a result, God was good to them (v. 20). Then there was Moses' mother, who hid her infant. When she could no longer hide him, she set him afloat on the Nile in a basket. No husband was mentioned when these decisions were made and carried out. Pharaoh's daughter discovered the infant and defied her father by adopting the child. Miriam, sister to Moses, who had followed the basket, resourcefully inquired if she could bring a wet nurse (Moses' mother) to feed the baby. When Moses was old enough, his mother brought him back to Pharaoh's daughter, and she finished raising him (vv. 1-10). All of these women acted on their own initiative, realizing that they risked a great deal by moving against the oppression of a male ruler.

Yet another woman, Moses' wife Zipporah, saved Moses' life by performing the priestly function of circumcision (Exod 4:24-26). Moses had just been called by God to release the Israelites from their bondage. He, Zipporah, and their son were on their way from Midian to Egypt. At one of the lodging places on their journey, "the Lord met him and tried to kill him." Moses apparently did nothing to defend himself. Instead, Zipporah, with incredible courage and quick wit, sought to placate God by circumcising their son. Her action directly confronted God's alleged intent to murder, and it saved Moses' life by using shed blood as a means of protection. Perhaps her action foreshadowed the Passover blood that later would be shed.[19]

God used these women of Exodus to bring about liberation from oppression for all of the Israelites. Their life-affirming decisions and actions led to the eventual inheritance of the Promised Land and forever altered the course of Judaism and Christianity.

Before they could claim this inheritance, some women who lived during the wandering in the wilderness stood up for themselves and claimed their personal inheritances. After the male Israelite leaders set up laws that prevented women from obtaining an inheritance, five women protested against it. The daughters of Zelophehad stood up to Moses and Eleazar the priest and argued that they deserved their father's inheritance, especially since they had no brothers. Moses went before the Lord to inquire as to what should be done. The Lord told Moses to grant the women their father's inheritance, and to continue that practice (Num 27:1-8).

Prophets and Wise Women

Prophets were those chosen to enter into the presence of God and then given divine authority to proclaim a particular message to God's people. Prophets took on the role of judge and corrector of priests who had gotten out of line (Isa 1:10-17; Jer 7; Amos 5:21-27). Unlike priests, the prophets had the unique right to proclaim, "Thus said the Lord . . ."[20] Prophets even selected kings and were sent to convict them of sin (1 Sam 10:1-16; 2 Sam 12:1-14). The prophets and the wise women were among the recognized leaders of the Old Testament (Jer 18:18).

Isaiah gives a detailed account of his calling in Isaiah 6. His experience involved a direct encounter with God and a particular commission to serve as a mouthpiece for God. Isaiah's wife was called a prophet (Isa 8:3). The writers of the Old Testament mentioned her and other women prophets without bringing any attention to the fact that they were women; it must have been generally assumed that God chose women as well as men to be mouthpieces for God and proclaimers of truth.

Miriam was both a prophet and a wise woman. She displayed uncanny wisdom when she asked Pharaoh's daughter if she needed a wet nurse for Moses. She was sent by God, along with Moses and Aaron, to deliver the Israelites from their Egyptian bondage (Micah 6:4). As prophet, she sang the Song of the Sea (Exod 15:20-21), which had been attributed to Moses and the people of Israel in a previous passage. There is only a fragment remaining in Exodus to tell of her important role as leader of the celebration; the fact that it is a small fragment leads scholars to believe it is an older, more original version of the song and story it told. This fragment has survived the centuries to stand as a witness to Miriam's authority to lead the Israelites as composer and singer. Through music, she proclaimed the activities of Yahweh at a pivotal time in Israelite history.

Deborah was another prophet who composed a song to proclaim the mighty works of Yahweh at a pivotal historical moment. She is perhaps the most well-known female in a leadership position in the Old Testament. Not only was she a prophet; she also was a judge over all of Israel and the top military commander for the nation (Jdgs 4:4-5:31). Her record was remarkably clean and free of blemish, especially considering those who followed after her. As judge, she was appointed to settle disputes among the Israelites, sort of like a Supreme Court justice. Solomon settled such a dispute in the famous story in 1 Kings 3:16-28. Solomon's great wisdom was heralded, and because Deborah served the Israelites in a similar function, we can probably assume she also had great wisdom.

When Deborah arrived on the scene in Judges 4, the northern part of Israel had been cruelly oppressed for about twenty years. The people lacked a strong political leader to take charge and change the situation. Apparently the Lord selected and then spoke directly to Deborah (Jdgs 4:6), because she sent for Israel's top military leader, Barak, and told him God would deliver the enemy into his hands. Barak agreed to fight the Canaanites, who had superior military might, but only on the condition that Deborah go as well, essentially naming her his commander-in-chief. He may well have wanted her along for her advice, for her recognized authority among the Israelites and her special relationship with the Lord. She agreed to go. After the victory, Deborah and Barak together sang a song of praise to God for their deliverance. Deborah had carried out the three functions that marked the ministry of Samuel: judge over Israel, prophet, and commissioner of military leaders. She used the power given to her, not to lord it over others but to empower others so that together they could achieve a mutual goal. God was pleased to use this woman in many leadership capacities and as a mouthpiece for God's messages.

A less widely known prophet was Huldah (2 Kgs 22:8-20; 2 Chron 34:14-28), who lived during the period when Jeremiah and Zephaniah were actively prophesying. The high priest at that time was Hilkiah. One day, Hilkiah found the book of the law in the house of the Lord. He had King Josiah informed, and when the book was read to the king, Josiah recognized that the people had not followed the law. King Josiah sent Hilkiah to inquire of the Lord about their fate. To make the inquiry, Hilkiah chose to seek out a prophet. For such an important message, he needed to make sure he contacted the right prophet. He chose Huldah and took several men with him to talk with her. Interestingly enough, the high priest did not seek out either the prophet Jeremiah or Zephaniah; he sought the wisdom and prophetic voice of a woman.

With great confidence, Huldah spoke to them with the formula, "Thus says the Lord," which revealed that her message came directly from God (2 Kgs 22:15, 18). The high priest, the king, and his cabinet apparently put great confidence in what Huldah prophesied to them, because they never questioned anything she said. She told them of the coming judgment, and she identified the book as the Word of God.

Through this proclamation, Huldah became the first person in the Bible to identify a particular work as the Word of God. This function was later given to men and called "canonization," or a process used to identify which writings were Holy Scripture and which were not.[21] Huldah's proclamation to the high priest and king made her the founder of biblical studies because she authorized God's Word.[22] Following Huldah's preaching, a great revival broke out among the people, and the king was able to institute several reforms.

The wisdom of Huldah was mirrored by three other wise women. Abigail showed her diplomatic skills and wisdom when she averted disaster from an angry David while he was fleeing King Saul (1 Sam 25). David and his men camped out on land belonging to Abigail and her husband Nabal, an action that had the effect of deterring robbery of sheep. David eventually sent some of his men to Nabal, seeking supplies. Nabal, whose name means "fool," sent David's men back empty-handed. Abigail, described by the writer as beautiful and intelligent, knew this meant David's men would be back, but not to make a request. She defied her husband's poor decision, acted independently, and sent supplies out to David. Hardly a submissive wife, Abigail saved her own life and that of her whole household—except for her husband. God blessed her for her wisdom and diplomatic skill.

The wise woman of Tekoa (2 Sam 14:2) performed the same role as Nathan had earlier. She told a story to David that led him to repentance, and he asked to have Absalom brought back. The wise woman of Abel Beth-maacah (2 Sam 20:16-22) negotiated a settlement that ended a revolt by a man named Sheba against David. She, too, spoke eloquently and was thereby able to save her city from destruction.

Another wise woman, though she is not labeled such, was the mother of King Lemuel. She gave an oracle to her son: Don't give away your strength to what destroys you. Don't pervert the rights of the afflicted. Give to those who need it. Speak up for the unfortunate. Judge righteously. Defend the rights of the afflicted and the needy (Prov 31:1-9). This woman was very interested in activism for justice and righteousness, and passed along those values to her son, who became a king.

A Woman of Song

One woman in the Old Testament who had no official leadership role still carries great significance for the role of women in church and society. She is the woman portrayed in the Song of Solomon.

Although there is debate as to whether this woman was a real person or whether she symbolized something, the fact that a woman in the Old Testament is portrayed in such a positive role is significant. The significance lies in the fact that she was able to live beyond the judgment given by God in Genesis 3. She was a woman of song—and had plenty to sing about. She knew that the so-called curse, which is actually only a description of the consequences of the fall, did not have to negatively affect relationship between women and men. She lived out a relationship of mutuality and equality with the man in the poem.

There are several ways the characters in the poem overcame the judgment. One contradiction to the so-called curse of Genesis 3:16 is the switch in who desired whom. In the Genesis account, the woman desired the man, and the man chose to rule her. In the Song, it is the man who desires the woman (7:10). The same Hebrew word for desire, *teshuqa,* is used. Here, it is the man who desires mutuality with the woman and a return to the bliss of the pre-Edenic fall. The desire to dominate the woman is missing altogether. Instead, it is replaced by the joy of mutuality.

In the creation account, when the man first called the woman (Gen 2:23), he did so to express delight in the mutuality and similarity he saw in the woman. The act of calling without naming expressed delight. Here, in the Song, the woman called the man as an expression of love and joy (1:1-4), not as an expression of power or dominance over him.[23] Neither was the woman submissive to the man, nor the man domineering toward her. The poem contains no sexism and no sex stereotyping; it is simply a celebration of love and sexuality. Together they were naked without fear or shame, just as in Eden (Gen 2:25). The love and joy they expressed toward each other was that of two people who became bone of bone and flesh of flesh (Gen 2:24).

The poem also mirrors Genesis 2:24 by showing the importance of the female side of the family, where the male leaves his family of origin to cleave to the woman. In the Song, only the mothers of both lovers are mentioned—a perfect seven times. The fathers are conspicuously absent (see Song 6:9; 8:5). It is the mother's house that carries importance, not the father's—which is never even mentioned. In addition, both references point to the wonder of birth, rather than to the pain of childbirth mentioned in Genesis 3:16.

Incidentally, this woman was never asked to bear children and was never called a wife. In fact, the idea of marriage is missing altogether. This was a very independent woman, who earned her own living as a shepherdess and as a keeper of vineyards. She took the lead in the poem by doing most of the speaking, thereby accepting a place of greater importance in the movement of the story than the man had.

In this poem, military images (1:9; 4:4; 6:4, 10; 7:4; 8:9, 10) and powerful animals (4:8) are used as symbols for the woman. These images, representing qualities of power, control, aggression, and strength, are generally considered masculine in Western culture. In this poem, however, they are used only for the female. For premonarchic Israelite society, this poem probably gives a glimpse of what rural life was like on the private level.

Other Women of Courage and Resourcefulness

In addition to Abigail, another woman diplomat surfaces in the Old Testament. Queen Esther rose from the lowly status of a Jewish woman orphan in postexilic Persia. She figured out how to work within the system she lived in to gain what she needed to survive and even to gain what she wanted. When her life and the lives of her people were threatened, she went through proper diplomatic procedures during a period of several days, including risking her own life, before making her request known to King Ahasuerus. Her process included three days of fasting and careful planning. Through her courage, she saved the lives of her people.

Ruth was another woman who demonstrated a radical kind of courage. She let go of everything that provided security in her culture—her opportunities for marriage within the context of her family of origin, her country with its familiarity, and her religion. Ruth had no possessions except her love for her mother-in-law Naomi when she set out for the uncertainty of a new country, a new religion, and almost certain poverty. Naomi and Ruth had no males to depend upon in a society where men owned all the property and all the means for making a living. Rather than look for a husband in her homeland, this Moabite woman chose to follow a widow even beyond the grave, moving into a land where her people were despised and told they could never become part of the Israelite community (see Deut 23:3-6). Her initiative and rare courage continued beyond the arrival in Naomi's homeland of Bethlehem. She initiated contact with Boaz, and careful planning with Naomi eventually landed Ruth a husband and Naomi a home for the rest of her days. When Ruth gave birth to a son, some women named the child and called him a son born to Naomi rather than to her deceased husband (4:7) or to Ruth's husband.

Another resourceful and remarkable Old Testament woman was the woman of Proverbs 31:10-31. She was known for her wisdom (v. 26) and did not behave as a silent, submissive wife. She was a businesswoman involved in farming, manufacturing, and real estate. She made major financial decisions and ran her family's household, a situation that placed the power of the household in her hands. She deserved the financial rewards of her labor and the honor due her for her efforts (v. 31).

God's Protection of Women

Not all women in the Old Testament were treated with respect. In fact, most of the time they were treated with disrespect. Rules were written by the males to exclude and devalue women. Women were used as property and given over to gang rapes (Gen 19; Jdgs 19:1-30). Yet this was not God's ideal. God does not force humans to follow a certain pattern. In fact, God gave humans such radical freedom, they crucified their Creator's only begotten son. Humans are limited by their ability to see what God wants. They are limited by such sins as pride, selfishness, and a lust for power. Humans have a limited capacity to receive revelation from God; and God works within human capacity and human willingness to follow.

Despite Old Testament society's treatment of women, God did provide women with some measure of protection. For example, the daughters of Zelophehad did receive their inheritance (Num 27:1-8). Women who were falsely accused of fornication or were victims of rape received some measure of protection (Deut 22:13-30). God also would not allow a jealous husband to judge his wife of adultery (Num 5:11-31). The period of uncleanness after childbirth (Lev 12:1-7) allowed women time to physically heal by protecting them from overly amorous husbands. And in a time when women were considered the ones at fault when no children were produced, Deuteronomy 7:14 makes it clear both women and men could be responsible for barrenness.

Women held positions of status and power in early Israelite society. Unfortunately, this began to change when the monarchy was established and public works were started. God allowed the monarchy as a concession to the people of Israel, and it spelled trouble for the women. The public sphere of Israelite life grew after the eleventh century B.C.E. Hierarchies developed, and so did the need for labor away from the family unit. Samuel described the change (1 Sam 8:11-13), explaining who the king would call to serve him. With the removal of certain important status-raising tasks from the household, and the parallel development of political and economic life, the status of women declined.[24]

Restrictions on their lives grew. Power shifted from the household, which was the primary social structure in early Israel, to male-dominated political and economic structures and the military. With a central political structure in place, Israelites began importing luxury items and ceramics. Men were already involved in production that could be exported, giving them more control over family economic resources.[25] The economic independence of the clan unit deteriorated, and production grew more centralized. Households were taxed, removing some of the economic decision-making power from the women.

As the centuries passed, the status of women continued to decline. When the second temple was built after the Exile, women were separated from the sacrificial area of the temple, revealing a significant drop in societal status. Many of the rabbinical writings from the centuries around the time of Christ were extremely negative toward women. The status of Jewish women in Palestine reached a significant low point when Christ appeared on the scene.

Questions for Reflection

1. How did the lives of Sarah, Rebekkah, and Rachel compare to those of women in premonarchic Israel? How much power and authority did they appear to have in their household units?

2. How is Hagar a model for homeless women? For women whose husbands abandon them and their children?
3. What role did water play in the events surrounding Miriam? (see Exod 2:1-10; 15:20-21; Num 20:1-2) How was this significant? What did nature do when Miriam died? (see Num 20:1-2)
4. What characteristics of Deborah's personality made her such a strong leader? Do you know other women who have these personality traits?
5. Ruth, a Moabite woman, was included in the Israelite community despite the Deuteronomic law forbidding it. Which groups of women where you live are excluded from your community? What can you do to include them?
6. Why do you think Huldah was the prophet of choice rather than Jeremiah or Zephaniah?
7. What characteristics describe Huldah's words and actions? Do you know other women with these characteristics?
8. What characteristics of Abigail's meeting with David make her an excellent role model for nonviolent peacemaking?
9. Why do you think the woman in the Song of Solomon is compared to military images and powerful animals? What characteristics do those images portray? Do those characteristics carry any significance for your life?
10. If you have a relationship with a significant other, how does the balance of power in your relationship compare with the balance between the woman and man in the Song of Solomon?
11. Why did women in early Israelite society have positions of influence and authority, but later did not? How does that make you feel?
12. Do you believe God gifted and called all of these women into leadership roles?
13. If you have a gift for wisdom, prophecy, or diplomacy, how do you believe God wants you to use it?

Notes

[1]Elisabeth Schüssler Fiorenza, *In Memory of Her* (New York: The Crossroad Publishing Co., Inc., 1983) 250.

[2]Bernadette J. Brooten, *Women Leaders in the Ancient Synagogue* (Chico CA: Scholars Press, 1982).

[3]Leonard Swidler, *Biblical Affirmations of Woman* (Philadelphia: Westminster Press, 1979) 100-105.

[4]Carol Meyers, *Discovering Eve* (New York: Oxford University Press, 1988) 166.

[5]Ibid., 51.

[6]Ibid., 56.

[7]Ibid., 60. Judges 5:18 and 2 Samuel 1:21 are better translated "terraced fields."

[8]Ibid., 61.

[9]Ibid., 146-47.

[10]Ibid., 156-57.

[11]Danna Nolan Fewell, *Gender, Power, and Promise* (Nashville: Abingdon Press, 1993) 9.

[12]Meyers, 169.

[13]Ibid., 41-42.

[14]Ibid., 181.

[15]Georges Barrois, "Women and the Priestly Office," in *Women and the Priesthood*, ed. Thomas Hopko (Crestwood NY: St. Vladimir's Seminary Press, 1983) 52.

[16]Elsa Tamez, "The Woman Who Complicated the History of Salvation," *New Eyes for Reading: Biblical and Theological Reflections by Women from the Third World*, ed. John S. Pobee and Barbel von Wartenberg-Potter (Oak Park IL: Meyer-Stone Books, 1987) 5-17.

[17]Savina J. Teubal, *Sarah the Priestess* (Athens OH: Swallow Press, 1984) 51.

[18]Gerda Lerner, *The Creation of Patriarchy* (New York: Oxford University Press, 1986) 168.

[19]Ilana Pardes, *Countertraditions in the Bible: A Feminist Approach* (Cambridge MA: Harvard University Press, 1992) 79-89.

[20]Gilbert Bilezikian, *Beyond Sex Roles: A Guide for the Study of Female Roles in the Bible* (Grand Rapids: Baker Book House, 1985) 69.

[21]Richard and Catherine Kroeger, *Women Elders . . . Sinners or Servants?* (New York: Council on Women and the Church of the United Presbyterian Church in the USA, 1981) 5.

[22]Leonard Swidler, *Biblical Affirmations of Woman* (Philadelphia: Westminster Press, 1979) 89.

[23]Phyllis Trible, *God and the Rhetoric of Sexuality* (Philadelphia: Fortress Press, 1978) 160.

[24]Meyers, 140.

[25]Ibid., 190, 192, 193.

Chapter 3

Jesus and Women

Mary Magdalene was not the "great sinner" of tradition. Jesus healed her by casting out seven demons (Luke 8:2), which probably indicated she had been mentally ill. Nothing in the Bible or from the writings of the early church fathers suggests she was a prostitute. Rather, through her strength of character and her understanding of Jesus, she became a leader among the women followers of Jesus. It was not until Augustine, in the fourth century, confused Mary Magdalene with Mary of Bethany (John 12:3) and the woman sinner (Luke 7:37) that she became equated with sin and sexual immorality. Mary Magdalene does not even show up in the Luke account until after the prostitute anoints Jesus.

Rather than being a symbol for unbridled sexuality, Mary Magdalene stands as a symbol for true discipleship. She was a follower of Jesus who stayed at the foot of the cross when the male disciples fled. She was the first witness to the resurrection of Jesus, and he commissioned her to proclaim the good news to the other disciples. In the apocryphal writings not included in the New Testament, she inspired the disciples to preach the good news. Her authority was reportedly great enough to create a controversy over what leadership roles she and Peter were to have.

During the Middle Ages, legend made Mary into a missionary saint of France. According to the story, she was driven out of Palestine and sailed to France, where she preached, converted, and baptized. Numerous stained-glass windows from that period depict her preaching. A sixteenth-century window in France shows her baptizing. Another window in Germany shows her consecrating Lazarus as bishop of Marseilles, thereby fulfilling priestly functions generally performed only by males.[1]

Jesus' treatment of Mary Magdalene as a valued human being—as more than "just a woman"—was revolutionary for that time in history. Unlike the people he lived among, Jesus never treated women as just mothers, wives, or housekeepers, or as inferior to men. He never degraded women or anything feminine nor called for the submission of women. He did not patronize women, speak condescendingly to them, shame them, or express anger at them.

Rather, Jesus treated women as full human beings, with rights and responsibilities, as intelligent people who could understand spiritual concepts and who had the right to learn as disciples. He provided a way for women to be admitted into the Christian community through the rite of baptism, which was open to both women and men. (The rite of passage into the Jewish community involved male-only circumcision.) Jesus presented no double standards regarding women and men. He did not discriminate against women. He took women seriously and answered their questions readily. The ministry of Jesus brought wholeness to numerous women. He showed them their worth and gave them dignity. These women would go on to risk societal conventions and even their own lives to follow this unusual man.

Mary Magdalene

Jesus brought wholeness to Mary Magdalene. Her deep devotion to Jesus and her courage probably emerged as a result. When Jesus cast the seven demons out of her life (Luke 8:2-3), he acknowledged that sometimes humans are overcome by oppressive powers. The coming of God's kingdom meant the overthrowing of those dehumanizing powers and the opportunity for wholeness. The number seven symbolized the completeness of her healing. Her response was to follow Jesus and to support him financially. Her ability to support Jesus financially indicates she was a woman of means, hardly the position of a prostitute in the ancient world—as Christian tradition has labeled Mary.

Not only did Mary Magdalene support Jesus and the disciples, she and the other women courageously followed Jesus around the countryside. Certainly such audacious behavior, following about after a company of men, could have brought judgment on their heads, especially because they had to leave their homes and families to do so. Nowhere were these women shown to need a man for anything, even though they lived in a culture that regarded women as inferior to and dependent on males.

Mary Magdalene is always mentioned first among the women followers of Jesus, indicating the other women followed her example, even to the point of putting their own lives at risk by standing beside the cross. They were well aware of the danger of appearing to be followers of a man being crucified as a political enemy of the state. There are reports that even those who cried at the scene of a crucifixion, or who showed up at the tomb of a crucified person, were themselves crucified.[2] The courage of these women stands in stark contrast to the fear of the male disciples, except for John, who fled for their lives. Ironically, at the scene where the body of Christ was broken and the blood of Christ was shed, the basis for the Eucharistic celebration, it was the women who were standing near; all of the men except John were not to be found.

Mary Magdalene was present at the burial of Jesus (Matt 27:59-61; Mark 15:46-47) and was the first to witness his resurrection (Matt 28:1-10; Mark 16:9; John 20:11-18). Jesus deliberately did not appear to the male disciples first. Rather, he waited until they left the tomb before he appeared to Mary Magdalene (John 20:1-18). She recognized him, and he responded by commissioning her to proclaim his resurrection to the other disciples. As primary witness to the resurrection of Christ, Mary Magdalene became the first apostle. She carried to the men the message that would become the most important teaching of the Christian faith (Acts 2:22-34), a message that revealed the foundation for Christianity, without which all preaching would be in vain (1 Cor 15:12-19).

The Bethany Sisters

While Mary Magdalene was the first person to witness the resurrection, Martha of Bethany was the first person to experience Jesus as the resurrection. Martha experienced Jesus as *the* resurrection when he raised her brother Lazarus from the dead. Several days earlier, while Lazarus was still sick, the sisters Martha and Mary of Bethany sent word to Jesus requesting his presence. Jesus tarried, and when he finally arrived, Lazarus had already been dead for four days. While Mary stayed at home, Martha went out to meet Jesus.

Martha's relationship with Jesus must have been solid, because she boldly accused Jesus of negligence for not showing up earlier: "Lord, if you had been here, my brother would not have died" (John 11:21). Yet even with the accusation, she spoke intelligently of faith: "Even now I know that God will give you whatever you ask of him" (v. 22). She did not yet know this would include the resurrection of her brother that very day.

Jesus then revealed for the first time—and to a woman—the focus of the Christian gospel: that Jesus is the resurrection and the life, and that those who believe in him will live even if they physically die.

Martha followed this announcement by speaking a confession of faith that paralleled Peter's renowned confession of faith in the synoptic Gospels. She and Peter used exactly the same words: "You are the Messiah, the Son of God" (John 11:27; Matt 16:15-19).

After making her historical confession, Martha went and called Mary, just as Andrew and Philip confessed faith and then called Peter and Nathaniel. Mary responded by coming, falling at Jesus' feet, and voicing the same accusation as Martha: "Lord, if you had been here, my brother would not have died."

Jesus felt deeply moved by the weeping of Mary and the others, and began weeping himself. Jesus then instructed that the stone be removed from Lazarus' tomb. The practical Martha still had not fully grasped what Jesus had said. Instead, she argued with him that the body was already rotting. After Jesus explained further, she relented, and Jesus raised Lazarus from the dead.

Following the resurrection of Lazarus, Jesus went to Bethany to stay with him and his two sisters. John said in 11:5 that Jesus loved Lazarus, Martha, and Mary. (No one else in the Gospels is directly said to be the object of Jesus' love, except for the Beloved Disciple in the Gospel of John.) Jesus had stayed with them before. Luke told about the time when Martha thoughtfully invited Jesus to stay in her home and a conflict arose between the sisters. The ever-responsible Martha was distracted, making preparations, doing the serving. Meanwhile, she felt resentful of her sister, who was sitting at Jesus' feet and listening.

Martha asserted herself, expressing what she believed was right. She lived the active life, the life of service and responsibility, fulfilling her duty to others. She was, after all, doing what any proper Jewish woman would do—her domestic duties. Mary, on the other hand, stayed where she was, doing what she believed was right—sitting at the feet of Jesus and learning from him. Mary must have sensed that her time with Jesus would be limited, and she wasn't about to waste that time on domestic duties.

Jesus pointed out that Mary was doing the one necessary thing, the good part—learning at the feet of Jesus. To sit at the feet of a teacher and learn was the activity of a disciple showing respect for a teacher, and this was a role commonly denied to women in that culture (John 7:16). Yet here, Jesus encouraged a woman to behave as a disciple.

Someone still had to do the serving, however. The second time Jesus stayed with Martha, Mary, and Lazarus, "they made him a supper." Apparently, Martha was not always stuck with all the work. The two sisters were no longer competing, but had worked out for themselves what was best. Jesus had, in fact, freed both women to be themselves, to do what each believed was right. Jesus freed them to be the individuals they were. Martha still did the serving. Perhaps she felt most comfortable with this role. The word used for serving is *diakonein,* the word used later by the church to represent Eucharistic table service, and even later used to describe the office of deacon. Martha was a true disciple in the sense that she served, as Jesus served.

Her sister Mary, on the other hand, chose another path of service. Taking on the role of a slave, she anointed the feet of Jesus. In her society, slaves washed guests' dusty, travel-worn feet. Mary followed their example, but instead of using water, she used a year's wages of pure nard, a perfume from India. Then she untied her hair and wiped Jesus' feet with it, an offering of great love and sacrifice. Only prostitutes in her society let down their hair in public; certainly no respectable woman would have behaved like that. Yet Mary let down her hair in front of a group of males, inciting conflict with them. Such behavior was uncharacteristic for the quiet, sensitive Mary. Apparently, Mary was no longer concerned about what others thought. She had learned to act on her own initiative, to "do her own thing," despite the disapproval of others. Strengthened by her interaction with Jesus, Mary had become an individual.[3]

Women Who Anointed Jesus

There are two other stories in the Gospels about women anointing Jesus, but the other two women are not mentioned by name. The woman in Luke 7:36-50 anointed Jesus' feet with tears and perfume. The woman in Matthew 26:6-13 and Mark 14:3-9 anointed Jesus' head with costly pure nard. These women acted assertively and boldly out of passionate feeling. They were scorned by men but blessed by Jesus.

The actions these women performed went far beyond what Jesus' hosts had failed to do. The woman in Luke washed Jesus' feet with her tears and dried them with her hair. A known prostitute, she made a public display by falling at Jesus' feet and then letting down her hair. She boldly disgraced not only herself but also Jesus. However, this woman must have sensed that Jesus would accept her deep expression of love and gratitude. She did not concern herself with what others thought; her only thought was of Jesus. Jesus, in response, showed the woman her value and worth in the eyes of God by forgiving her.

The woman in Matthew and Mark anointed Jesus' head with very costly nard, representing a year's worth of labor. Her action carried two significant messages. First, she acted as a prophet when she anointed Jesus, just as Old Testament prophets anointed kings (1 Sam 10:1; 16:12-13). Standing over the head of Jesus and pouring perfume on his head, she was the first to declare his lordship. This woman, in her wisdom, saw Jesus for who he was and made her proclamation in the midst of a company of men who still did not understand. Through this act of consecration, she helped prepare him for his upcoming task.[4]

Second, the woman anointed Jesus for his burial. Although even the twelve disciples did not see what was coming for Jesus, this wise woman did, and she anointed him in preparation. Usually, bodies were anointed after death as a sign of reverence; but here, this woman wanted to worship and comfort Christ in preparation for his impending death. She may have been the first to know that following Christ would lead to crucifixion and death. This woman anointed a king who would die and a king who would rule despite the Roman occupation of Israel. Just as Jesus had so often done himself, this woman turned the way of the world on its head, introducing new values. One of those new values was a woman taking on a traditionally male role of anointing a king (2 Sam 2:4).[5]

This woman probably paid dearly for her actions. She may have spent her life's savings on the perfume. If she were married, her husband most likely would not have understood her actions, and probably would have divorced her for them. This woman might well have faced a future of societal disgrace and economic hardship. Jesus gave her a gift in response—the knowledge that her deed would always be remembered.

Joanna

Another woman who paid dearly to follow Jesus was the disciple Joanna. She is mentioned only briefly among the women followers of Jesus (Luke 8:1-3), but that tiny piece of information speaks volumes. Joanna was the wife of Chuza, Herod's steward.

What man of Herod's court—a royal minister of finance—would stand for his wife traipsing about the countryside with a ragtag band of rural folk, following a radical preacher who behaved in shocking ways? Not only that, but this woman did not know when to be discreet about her association with this insurrectionist named Jesus. While Nicodemus secretly came to Jesus by night (John 3:1-2), Joanna stood by the cross of a condemned traitor by day and came in the daylight to Jesus' tomb (Luke 23:49, 55). In return for her faithfulness, she became one of the women rewarded with the first knowledge of the resurrection of Jesus. She and the other women were given the commission to tell the other disciples that Jesus had risen from the dead (Luke 24:1-10).

Joanna had left not only her wealthy husband but also all the advantages of court life to follow Jesus. She left family and influence, although she continued to have enough wealth to help support the disciples and Jesus. She may well have provided the seamless robe Jesus wore, as well as a comfortable location for the Last Supper—things fishermen's wives could not have supplied.[6]

Perhaps the reason Joanna left her whimsical court life was because Jesus healed her, either of evil spirits or of sickness. She had discovered something her court life and marriage to an important political figure could not give her, and she was assertive enough to leave it behind for a more meaningful life. Joanna hardly behaved like an obedient or submissive wife, and Jesus never rebuked her for her actions and courage.

Salome

Joanna was not the only woman who left her husband to follow Jesus. Salome and her two sons, James and John, left Zebedee to follow the itinerant preacher. Her family was apparently wealthy enough to hire servants to help with the fishing (Mark 1:20), so she left behind her physical comforts and security.

Salome is perhaps best known for her request of Jesus, that he place her two sons at his right and left hands in his kingdom (Matt 20:20-28). This mother was doing what any loving Jewish mother would do: asking for something for her children to improve their lives. As a Jewish woman, much of her stature in society depended on the stature of the males in her family. These women lived through their children. So, despite having abandoned one societal value—her marriage—in another way, she still clung to her society's view of what was important—positions of power. Her understanding of the call of Christ was still immature at this point.

We can view this incident from another angle, however. Either her sons asked Salome to make this request of Jesus, or she did it on her own initiative. Either way, this was an acknowledgment of the good standing she had with Jesus and his accessibility to women. She served as a liaison for her sons, sons who certainly were not shy—being nicknamed "sons of thunder."

Later, Salome reached maturity and individuality. When Jesus hung on the cross, at least one of her sons fled. (Her son John stayed, as reported in the Gospel he wrote.) Salome, however, did not flee. She stayed in the vicinity of the cross, watching despite the possibility of arrest for being associated with the alleged criminal. Her strength of character, revealed in her willingness to stay, indicated she was no longer dependent upon society's views of a woman's place. Her contact with Jesus enabled her to become a full person, making and acting upon her own choices.

Mary, the Mother of Jesus

Another woman who was not dependent upon society's view of her was Mary the mother of Jesus. With God's blessing, she acted as her own person, making hard choices. When God sent an angel to her to announce the coming of the Messiah, she agreed to an arrangement that would essentially leave her open to being stoned for fornication.

God asked a single woman to carry and bear a child, breaking moral family values with this request. God also broke societal conventions when God did not send the angel to seek permission from Mary's father or from Joseph, her betrothed. Instead, God sent the angel directly to Mary, bypassing what a normal Jew would have expected. In addition, it was Mary who fed and nourished the body of Christ during nine months of pregnancy. It was Mary who gave him birth, bringing forth the body and blood of the Christ, shedding her own blood and risking her own life in the process.

Mary did not shrink from doing what needed to be done. At the wedding in Cana, Jesus addressed Mary as "Woman," using what was then a term of polite respect.[7] In response, she gave orders to the servants and expected them to be followed. Jesus, in turn, did as she wanted him to do and made sure there was plenty of wine so the hosts of the wedding were not left embarrassed. Mary acted as an assertive, strong woman who knew what was needed and made sure those needs were met. She was socially responsible to her hosts and was treated with respect by Jesus, who submitted to her wishes.

At the end of Jesus' ministry, Mary courageously stood at the foot of the cross. In so doing, she stood as a true disciple of Jesus, one of his true followers.

The Samaritan Woman

One woman who started a following of Jesus among non-Jews was the Samaritan woman. This woman dared to talk with Jesus in public, responding to his need for water. Jesus perceived her need for healing. She had lived with five husbands, which probably meant she had experienced a great deal of grief and loss in her adult life. Because men could divorce their wives but women could not leave their husbands, she may well have been abandoned or divorced, or the men may all have died. Jesus was aware of her losses and her current life situation. She may have chosen simply to live with the sixth man because a sixth marriage may have been too much for her to bear. In any case, it is unlikely she was the town harlot, as tradition has made her out to be, because the townspeople listened to her when she came to tell them about Jesus. They would have laughed at her if she had a reputation for prostitution. Her reputation must have been intact enough for the Samaritan villagers to take her seriously.

Jesus took her seriously as well, even though she was a woman and a Samaritan. Men considered it unseemly to talk to women in public (John 4:27), especially about theological issues. The Jews also considered Samaritan women perpetually unclean, because they believed these women menstruated from the cradle.[8] The woman herself, as well as the disciples, was shocked by Jesus' behavior (4:9, 27). The fact that the disciples said nothing to Jesus about their surprise indicates they had seen him behave in unconventional ways before this encounter. They must have known that any challenge to the egalitarian practices of Jesus would not be favorably received.

Not only did Jesus break with societal conventions by talking with the Samaritan woman; he also had the longest private conversation recorded in the Bible. He revealed profound spiritual truths to her: that God is Spirit, that Jesus is the living water and the source of eternal life, and that she was to worship in spirit and truth. Perhaps most important, though, Jesus revealed to her that he was the Messiah, saying it for the first time and saying it to a Samaritan woman. The woman's response was a confession of faith she spoke to her neighbors: "He cannot be the Messiah, can he?" (4:29) Her confession came long before Peter's confession in John 6:69. Her words to the villagers also were seeds sown that would later be harvested by others. She might well be described as the first missionary to the Samaritans, who had Gentile blood.

By treating the Samaritan woman with respect—talking with her in the open, talking with her even though she was a Samaritan, and revealing profound spiritual truths to her—Jesus let her know she was valued by God. He restored her dignity and wholeness, looking beyond her grief and brokenness to her worth and value as a child of God.

The Syro-Phoenician Woman

One woman who knew the inherent worth and value of herself and her daughter pleaded for the restoration of her child, and Jesus responded by granting her wish. This woman really had no right to expect anything from Jesus. She had four strikes against her: (1) She was racially a Syro-Phoenician. (2) She was culturally Greek. (3) She was a woman. (4) Apparently, she had no husband, son, or male relative on whom to rely or who could act on her behalf (Mark 7:24-30;

Matt 15:21-28). She was probably a widow, a position that placed her near the bottom of the social scale. All this didn't stop her; she knew what she wanted, and she argued impressively for it. She not only spoke in public to a male, but she shouted. She cried out enough to bother and probably embarrass the disciples, who implored Jesus to dismiss her. Jesus, in the meantime, was probably exhausted from his recent incursions with the Pharisees and other Israelites, and needed to escape for a time from the demanding crowds.

This woman would not be put off. In her desperate persistence, she made her way to Jesus and fell at his feet, begging him to heal her daughter. Jesus was not prepared to deal with her; he was on retreat. He had more than he could handle just moving among the Jewish people; in human form, there wasn't the time or energy to deal with Gentiles as well. That would come later when the apostles would spread the gospel abroad. He turned this woman down, making it clear his work was only among the Jews.

The Syro-Phoenician woman refused to take no for an answer. She matched her wits with Jesus, courageously entering into theological debate with the Son of God. She insisted that even the crumbs were good enough for her and her daughter. Jesus saw her determination to get her needs met, even if it meant offending others. Unlike the rest of those in his culture, Jesus did not rebuff her or tell her to be silent, submissive, or obedient. Rather, he rewarded her assertiveness by granting her desire.

The Syro-Phoenician woman is the only person in the Bible who won an argument with Jesus, and that argument was a request for Jesus to extend the banquet table of God to the Gentiles. This single mother's personal wholeness led to the healing of her daughter.

Women Healed by Jesus

When Jesus healed Jairus' daughter, raising her from the dead, he held her by the hand (Mark 5:22-24, 35-43). In contrast, Jesus did not physically touch the widow of Nain's son or Lazarus when he raised them from the dead. To touch a corpse was to make oneself unclean in Jewish society at that time (Num 19:11, 13), yet Jesus ignored the taboo in the case of a girl.

He also ignored the taboo against touching a menstruating woman (Lev 15:25-30). A woman, who had suffered from a hemorrhage for twelve years, broke through the crowd to touch Jesus' garment in the hope of being healed (Matt 9:20; Mark 5:25; Luke 8:43-44). Jesus felt power leave his body when she touched him, and he asked, "Who touched my clothes?" The woman grew frightened because she knew by touching Jesus, she had defiled him. But with courage, integrity, and honesty, she revealed herself. By speaking up, she revealed her condition to those around her, suffering their disdain. She also risked the wrath of this itinerant preacher whom she had made unclean.

Yet Jesus, rather than make her feel guilty and ashamed for her actions and bodily condition, spoke to her with affection: "Daughter, your faith has made you well; go in peace, and be healed of your disease." This woman experienced the healing love of God not only for her physical illness but also for her shame and guilt. She walked away with peace in her life, because she had been made whole on every level of her being. She experienced the great worth and dignity Jesus bestowed upon her.

Another woman Jesus healed was a cripple (Luke 13:10-17). He approached this woman who could not even look up to see her coming Savior. When Jesus was challenged for healing this woman on the Sabbath, Jesus responded by calling the woman a daughter of Abraham. Until then, the only reference to the spiritual heirs of Abraham was to males, never to females.[9] Here, Jesus made it clear that women had just as much of a right to the spiritual inheritance of Abraham as any male had.

Women Disciples

While Jesus made it clear that women could share in the spiritual inheritance of the Jewish race, he did not invite any women to join his inner circle of disciples. Why?

Given the society Jesus lived in, it would have been practically impossible for a woman to be part of an inner circle of disciples. To have invited women into his inner circle would have invited scandal, which would have severely damaged his mission. It was already extremely radical for Jesus to have women following him as disciples and meeting his financial needs. Note, however, that neither did Jesus select any Gentile men for his inner circle of disciples. Jesus did work within the culture he found himself in, and he limited himself to a very small population of people. He would come to depend on his disciples to spread the news abroad.

Those disciples did include women. Jesus allowed women "to follow" and "to serve" him. These activities were the equivalent of discipleship. In Mark 15:40-41, women *akolouthein* ("followed"), *diakonein* ("served," from which the church gets the word deacon), and *synanabasai* ("came up with") Jesus; these were the technical terms for discipleship (see also Matt 27:55).

The word "to follow" indicates full discipleship (see Mark 2:14; Matt 8:19-22; Luke 5:27-28). These women understood that to follow Jesus was to serve; this was something the male disciples did not yet understand. The final term, *synanabasai,* is repeated in Acts 13:31, connecting the followers of Jesus with those who were his witnesses.[10] Interestingly, in the account of those following Jesus found in Luke 8:1-3, it only includes the twelve male disciples and a group of "many" women. And just as Jesus' inner circle of disciples consisted of three men, here three women disciples are specifically named.

Full discipleship meant taking up a cross and following Jesus (Mark 8:34; 10:28). To take up their crosses meant they were willing to be crucified for following Jesus. It was the women disciples who took up their crosses to follow Jesus, proving to be Jesus' true disciples during his crucifixion and burial. Judas betrayed him, Peter denied him, and the rest of the men fled (except John). Yet, these women disciples stood by, continued to follow, and did not flee in terror from the possibility of arrest and execution for following a condemned man. They were faithful to the bitter and highly dangerous end . . . and their faithfulness was rewarded with the first news of the new beginning. Even after the resurrection, the women are shown as believing while the men are shown as unconvinced.

These women followers of Jesus understood what it meant to be healed and to become whole persons through contact with Jesus. They had become strong, courageous individuals who assertively lived out their convictions. These women understood in their daily lives what it meant to feel and believe in their own dignity and worth given to them by God.

Questions for Reflection

1. Why is it okay in many denominations for only men to consecrate and serve the Eucharist or Lord's Supper, when it was a woman who first presented the body and the blood of Christ when she gave birth to Jesus, and it was women who were in close proximity when Christ's body was broken and his blood shed on Calvary?
2. Compare the call of Mary Magdalene (John 20:11-18) with the call of Paul (Acts 9:1-20; 22:6-16; 26:9-18).
3. How did Mary Magdalene's recognition of Jesus at the resurrection (John 20:16) tie in with Jesus saying that he calls his sheep by name, and they hear his voice and follow him (John 10:1-18)? What does this say about Mary Magdalene?
4. What might the broken alabaster vial symbolize for the woman who anointed Jesus?
5. Why would Jesus ignore the taboo to touch a girl who had died, but would not touch men who had died?
6. What other positive characteristics do you see in the Syro-Phoenician woman, Mary the mother of Jesus, Mary Magdalene, and Joanna?
7. Which of the women mentioned in this chapter make good role models for other women? Why?
8. What qualities do these women share?
9. If members of your church do not currently follow a servant style of leadership, what would happen if they did? In what ways would your congregation change and/or benefit?
10. Jesus did not respond immediately to the desperate needs of the Syro-Phoenician woman. Do you expect instantaneous results when you turn to God for help?If you don't get quick results, what do you do?

Notes

[1]Elisabeth Moltmann-Wendel and Jürgen Moltmann, *Humanity in God* (New York: The Pilgrim Press, 1983) 5-11.

[2]Luise Schottroff, *Let the Oppressed Go Free: Feminist Perspectives on the New Testament* (Louisville KY: John Knox Press, 1993) 171-72.

[3]Ibid., 57.

[4]Ibid., 95-98.

[5]Ibid.

[6]Ibid., 133-39.

[7]Lecture notes from New Testament class taught by David Garland, The Southern Baptist Theological Seminary, Louisville KY, 1986.

[8]Leonard Swidler, *Biblical Affirmations of Woman* (Philadelphia: Westminster Press, 1979) 189.

[9]Alvin J. Schmidt, *Veiled and Silenced: How Culture Shaped Sexist Theology* (Macon GA: Mercer University Press, 1989) 174.

[10]Elizabeth M. Tetlow, *Women and Ministry in the New Testament* (New York: Paulist Press, 1980) 97.

Chapter 4

Jesus' Good News for Women

According to legend, Martha of Bethany, her sister, and Mary Magdalene were exiled from the Holy Land, placed in a rudderless boat, and left to die at sea. They survived, however, and landed in what is now France. There, Martha preached and performed acts of healing. One man who came to hear her preach had to cross a river on his way there, and he drowned. Martha responded by raising him from the dead, fulfilling her apostolic role.

In another legend, roughly parallel to that of St. George and the dragon, Martha defeated her own dragon. Her method, in contrast to the violence of St. George, was peaceful. With bare feet and wearing a robe, rather than spurs and armor, she simply set a cross before the dragon and sprinkled it with holy water, rather than lancing it after a long battle. In the end, St. George killed his dragon, but Martha subdued hers. Martha's method symbolized the redemption of evil, rather than simply its destruction. Martha moved from victim to victor over evil, working with the power of God rather than using the power of violence.[1]

It seems fitting that legend would give Martha, the first person to learn that Jesus is the resurrection, the honor of raising a man from the dead and redeeming evil through the power of God. In the New Testament, Martha probably is best known for her service. It was she who served as hostess when Jesus went to stay with her, her sister Mary, and their brother Lazarus.

Jesus himself came to be a servant: "For the Son of Man came not to be served but to serve, and to give his life a ransom for many" (Mark 10:45; see also Matt 20:26-28; Mark 10:42-44; Luke 22:25-27). He emphasized repeatedly that the first would become the last, and the last would become first in the Kingdom of God (Matt 19:30; 20:16; Mark 10:31; Luke 13:30; 22:26-27). Jesus' earthly journey was the ultimate model for the servant role of leaders in the Christian community. Jesus related to and served those who were considered the least in his culture—women (especially widows and prostitutes), slaves, and children—because these people had no religious or political power in the Jewish community.[2] Prostitutes were generally poor women who had no marketable skills and so found this "profession" their only means of survival.[3]

Jesus taught women in the Court of Women, unlike other teachers of his day. He used examples of women in his stories and included women among his most faithful disciples. Jesus encouraged children to come to him (Matt 18:1-6). He took on the role of a house slave when he washed the disciples' feet (John 13:4-5, 12-17). He was sold to the chief priests for thirty pieces of silver (Matt 26:14-16), the price for a slave. He later died like a treasonous criminal.

His death symbolized the ultimate sacrifice necessary for the birth of the Christian community. He died to liberate individuals from their sins and to show that power is made perfect in weakness. When Jesus died, he died to end relationships of dominance and submission based on power or powerlessness (Matt 20:26-28). Jesus' power was the power to empower others, not to lord it over them. Jesus' example of how properly to use power involved enabling others to exercise their rights and freedoms.

Jesus not only behaved as a servant; he also used symbols to express this idea to his followers. Perhaps the best illustration of servant leadership comes from Jesus' reference to himself as a mother hen (Isa 31:5; Luke 13:34; Matt 23:37). A mother hen is hardly the symbol for the type of leadership generally thought of in Western culture—it seems more laughable to some people than a serious role model. A mother hen, however, represents a single parent caring for her young. The mother hen is a servant to her chicks when she provides them with protection, strength, guidance, lovingkindness, and gentleness.[4] Through her care, the chicks will grow up to be strong and healthy. To be a true leader in the kingdom of God is to be like a mother hen.

Jesus made another significant reference to himself as a nurturing mother figure. He said, "Let the one who believes in me drink." The only way one can drink from another human being is through a nursing mother. Jesus strengthened this image by continuing, "As the scripture has said, 'Out of the believer's heart shall flow rivers of living water' " (John 7:37). The Greek word for "heart" is *koilia,* a word that refers to the "hidden, innermost recesses of the human body." Some scholars refer to *koilia* as the heart,[5] and a mother's milk is produced on both sides of the heart. Most mothers who have nursed their children understand on a deep level the sense of security, comfort, and nurturance they give their infants while breastfeeding.

Women as Equals

The figures of mothers, as well as sisters and brothers, played a role in the new family of equals Jesus came to establish. In a world dominated by men, where women were expected to submit to their husbands and adopt their religions, Jesus brought a faith in which women could hold places of equality with men, as mothers and sisters and brothers. Jesus never set up hierarchies among his followers, and he resisted those who tried to establish power structures (see Matt 20:20-28). His teachings reflected his interest in seeing that all people were treated equally.

God established this interest in the Old Testament. Under the original covenant, the people of God were to function under God's authority, not that of another human. As time went on, though, humans found the arrangement unsatisfactory. They wanted a more visible and centralized authority structure. When the Hebrews needed human leadership to escape from slavery in Egypt, God provided a team: Moses, Aaron, and Miriam (Mic 6:4). When the Hebrews entered the Promised Land, the Lord raised up judges to provide leadership (Jdgs 2:16-18). The Hebrews did not find this satisfactory either, so they called for a monarchy, in violation of God's desires. God granted their wish anyway (1 Sam 8:7; 10:19; 12:17-25). Generally, human authority figures did not work out well for the Hebrews, and in the case of the monarchy led to the oppression of the poor and those living in the rural areas. The prophets continually fought against the oppression of the powerful over the powerless, especially in view of the fact that the Hebrews were a people released from the bondage of Egypt. The prophet Micah called for the return of peace and egalitarianism, where each person could make a living and not be afraid (Mic 4:4).

When Jesus walked among the people, he did not set up hierarchies among his followers. When Jesus referred to Peter as the rock upon which he would build the church, he designated Peter as an important founder of the early church community. Later Peter himself acknowledged that the true foundation of the church was not himself, but Jesus (1 Pet 2:4-6).

Jesus came to establish a church of equals, a church that included women on an equal status with men. The disciples were to become a family—Jesus' true family. Jesus' family included mothers and sisters and brothers who do the will of God (Mark 3:31-35). In this family, note that one member is missing—the father. This was highly significant in the ancient world. At the time of Jesus, families were ruled by one man, called a *pater familias* ("father of the family"). This man held the power of the state in his household, with the right to execute members of the family for disobeying him. He reigned with the power of life and death in his hands,[6] and members of his household were to worship whomever he worshiped.[7] The lowliest and most oppressed in this society were the women, especially widows and prostitutes. They were poor and marginalized, having no status or dignity. Yet they were the ones Jesus helped and whom he taught would enter the kingdom of heaven first.[8]

Jesus, familiar with this family setup, came to establish a new kind of family, a family without power structures or patterns of dominance and oppression. Jesus encouraged his followers to leave behind their loyalties to families that were based on power structures and dominance-submission relationships (Matt 10:37-38; Luke 14:26) to become disciples and form a new family (Mark 3:31-35). The father of this household would be God (Matt 23:9). The followers of Jesus were to be his mother and sisters and brothers. Members of the household of God were to serve each other as equals. This radical break with the family structure familiar to the disciples provided a new model for relationships, not based on the prevalent dominance-submission relationships, but based on relationships of mutuality and equality.[9]

Christians were no longer to refer to anyone but God as father (Matt 23:9), which means they were no longer to be subject to another human's wielding of power.[10] This did not mean that earthly fathers could not be included in the Christian community; they simply had to relinquish the power and status they held within their family units.[11] That power and status belongs to God, who acts as the loving father in the new family.[12] The role of father played by God would be like the father of the prodigal son—a father who does not dominate, rule, or punish. Rather, this father respects human freedom, is patient, misses us when we stray, forgives us of everything, and runs to embrace us upon our return.[13] It is the relationship Jesus had with God, whom he called "Abba" (Mark 14:36). Abba was a term of endearment and affection used by adults with their beloved fathers, indicating a relationship of trust and respect.[14] When Jesus told his disciples they were no longer servants but friends (John 15:15), which made them equals, then they also were given a new relationship to Abba, the loving parent.

Jesus officially instituted this new family when he was on the cross, telling his mother that the Beloved Disciple was her son, and telling the Beloved Disciple that Mary was his mother. Even Jesus' mother had to form a new relationship to Jesus' family of equals, relinquishing her old ties.

Women and Spiritual Truths

As part of encouraging the formation of a family of equals, Jesus chose to teach women as well as men. Unlike his contemporaries, Jesus taught in locations where women had access to his message, such as in people's homes, out in the open countryside, and in the Court of Women in the Temple (Luke 21:1-4). Jesus taught Mary of Bethany in her home and taught Martha of Bethany at a tomb site. Jesus talked easily with women, answering their questions and providing theological instruction.

Jesus revealed deep spiritual truths to women. He told the Samaritan woman he was the Messiah, the source of living water for eternal life; that she was to worship in spirit and in truth; and that God is Spirit (John 4). He told Martha of Bethany he is the resurrection and the life (John 11). He told Mary Magdalene he had risen from the dead.

Jesus also taught concerning situations directly involving women in their relationships with men. In Jewish society, adultery was considered a crime against the male, not the female, because the offspring would inherit the man's property. If a wife had a child by someone who was not her husband, this child would violate the husband's property rights.[15] Such a violation was so damaging to the male point of view that capital punishment (stoning) was used as a deterrent. Jesus taught that men could commit adultery even against a woman who had no husband (Matt 5:28), which revealed that women had rights, too, and could be harmed by adultery.

When the scribes and Pharisees caught a woman committing adultery and brought her to Jesus, they asked him if she should be stoned. Jesus turned the tables on the men and asked them if they were themselves without sin (John 8:3-11). Jesus helped them recognize their double standard, made more ridiculous because if the woman had been caught in the very act of adultery, there had to be a man with her; and, according to ancient laws, both men and women committing adultery were subject to stoning (Lev 20:10). Why was the man who committed adultery with her not brought before Jesus to be stoned? Jesus refused to place all the blame on the woman. Instead, he told her to go and sin no more. He broke Old Testament law and taught her that she did not have to carry all the blame, that she was a woman worthy of life.

When it came to marriage, Jesus taught that women and men had equal responsibilities and rights. Among Jesus' contemporaries, the rabbis had two schools of thought concerning divorce. According to one group, unchastity was the sole reason men could divorce. In the other school of thought, men could divorce their wives for minor offenses.[16] Two matters made the situation worse for women in the first century. First, the Jews believed God granted men the right to have more than one wife (see Exod 21:10; Deut 21:15-17).[17] Second, women could not divorce their husbands; only men could divorce their wives.

In response, Jesus affirmed monogamy as God's will for people (Matt 19:3-12; Mark 10:3-5). Jesus made it clear that both the man and the woman had the right to divorce (Mark 10:11-12). Yet Jesus did not approve of divorce. Despite the fact that Old Testament law given by Moses allowed for divorce (Deut 24:1-4), Jesus emphasized that the intent of God was monogamy and equality within marriage.

Jesus moved beyond the written law to the intent of God as reflected in the very creation of male and female. Referring to both creation stories, Jesus focused only on the equality of male and female expressed in both accounts. Jesus repeated that male and female are both made in the image of God (Gen 1:27), and that when male and female join together they become one flesh (Gen 2:24). When two become one flesh, one cannot dominate the other because they are one and the same.

Jesus had to remind the Pharisees that men and women were created to share a relationship of mutuality and equality in marriage.

Jesus never told men how to rule their wives, and he never told wives to submit to their husbands. To substantiate this radical departure from the views of his culture, Jesus included, among his followers, women who had left their husbands behind. Jesus did not come to affirm that men could dominate women, or that women were to subject themselves to their husbands, as the second creation account is often interpreted. In fact, the above two positive references are the only times Jesus mentioned the creation accounts. Jesus never referred to the judgments made on the man or the woman in the Garden of Eden. After all, Jesus came to redeem humanity, not to punish for or perpetuate the mistakes of the past.

Nowhere did Jesus ever mention or refer to the judgment that women were to experience pain in childbirth (Gen 3:16). Instead, Jesus used the profound feminine experience of childbirth as a positive metaphor for people who are spiritually reborn (John 3:1-21) and as a metaphor for the disciples' coming grief and pain that would then turn into joy (John 6:16-22).

While Jesus acknowledged the depth of meaning and the dignity of childbirth, he did not see that as the sole focus of a woman's life. This view of women as wombs and breasts was prevalent in Jesus' day. Take, for example, the woman who cried out to Jesus, "Blessed is the womb that bore you and the breasts that nursed you" (Luke 11:27-28). She clearly placed her values on procreation and nurturing children. Jesus challenged this widespread idea by pointing out that hearing and obeying God should be the primary focus of life.

Women in the Parables

To more effectively teach the women he spoke to, Jesus taught using stories with women in them and stories about things women could easily understand and relate to. This was highly unusual at the time. The rabbis did not use women in their illustrations or for their examples when they taught, unless the examples were negative.[18] Jesus, the master storyteller, included stories about and of interest to women.

In one parable, Jesus used a woman to illustrate the importance of praying and not giving up. The story involved a widow who actively sought justice (Luke 18:1-5). This woman understood the law well enough to know she was right, and she took action. She courageously went to the judge and implored him enough times that he would no longer say "no" to her request. This feisty woman had a goal, and she achieved it through her persistence. She was hardly submissive, nor did she play the role of victim. She was outspoken, exhibited strength of character, and was not concerned about her image. She asserted her rights repeatedly until she received the protection she needed.

Even more remarkable was the parable Jesus told using a poor woman to represent God. Jesus compared the woman who hid leaven in flour to God (Matt 13:33; Luke 13:21). Scholars know she was a poor or slave woman because in rural areas women baked the bread, and such women were generally poor or were slaves. In the city, men produced bread commercially.[19]

The parable about the woman who hid leaven in flour has more than one level of meaning. First, leaven represents something that is small, insignificant, or hidden.[20] Jesus indicated that even though women were considered insignificant in the religious life of his culture, their impact could be great, just as the impact of the seemingly insignificant leaven on flour can be great. When women are compared to the kingdom of heaven, they are participants in the salvation of the world. It is clear this bakerwoman is being compared to God, because in the parallel passage (Matt 13:31-32; Luke 13:18-19), the man sowing the seeds also is compared to God.

A second interpretation reveals even more impact for women. In Jesus' culture, unleavened bread was used during the Passover to signify God's authority. In contrast, in rabbinical writings leaven represented sin. The rabbis believed leaven caused things to decay, so they used it as a symbol for human corruption and evil.[21] Jesus echoed this idea in his teachings about the leaven of King Herod and the Sadducees and Pharisees (Mark 8:15). In this parable about the woman who hid leaven in flour, however, Jesus reversed the symbols. He used leaven to represent not evil, but the kingdom of God. In a shocking statement sure to catch the attention of those listening, Jesus used something associated with evil—leaven—to transform the world. Similarly, women, who in his culture were associated with evil (they blamed Eve for initiating the fall and thereby bringing evil into the world), are shown in this parable providing a source of salvation (the growth of the kingdom of God).[22] This second interpretation is substantiated by Jesus' teachings following this parable, where he taught that those who were not expected to receive salvation would indeed receive it. Jesus had shown his followers the powerful life-changing ability of women to transform the world when there was a little bit of the kingdom of heaven in their midst.

A short while later, Jesus followed up with parallel sayings about two people who are compared to God. This is clear from the similar endings of both stories, in which there is great celebration in heaven over the one thing lost and then found. The first image is masculine, represented by a shepherd (Luke 15:3-7). The second image is feminine, represented by a woman householder (vv. 8-10). Jesus told the story of a woman who had ten coins but lost one and swept the whole house looking for it. This woman was not shown in relation to any man. Rather, she owned her own money, and therefore her own power—which was not the normal woman's experience in ancient Palestine. This woman also was assertive and persistent in finding what was rightfully hers. Next, Jesus compared this woman searching for a lost coin to God seeking repentance from sinners. Jesus openly compared the activity of God to the activity of a woman, even though his audience included Pharisees and scribes, men who sometimes grouped women with tax collectors and sinners.[23]

When this analogy is read with the preceding and the following analogies, one comes up with an interesting situation. The first story, about the shepherd searching for the lost sheep, is an analogy for Jesus. The third story is a parable about God the Father awaiting the return of the prodigal son. Here, two members of the Trinity are represented, and sandwiched between them is a third analogy about God, told as a woman seeking a lost coin. Perhaps this middle story about a woman represents the Holy Spirit. It has certainly been so interpreted at various times in church history, because some early Christian art depicts the Holy Spirit as a woman.[24]

By using women as positive role models in his parables and by teaching profound theological truths to women, Jesus gave women dignity and worth within the new family of equals he was creating. Jesus wanted women to understand that they were of as much value as men in the eyes of God. After all, Jesus came to give abundant life (John 10:10) not only to men but also to women. The abundant life includes becoming mature people.

Jesus told his followers, "Be perfect, therefore, as your heavenly Father is perfect" (Matt 5:48). The word translated "perfect" is *teleios.* When used in reference to people, *teleios* means "of age full-grown, mature, adult . . . perfect, fully developed in a moral sense."[25] Jesus wanted these women to become mature. This idea was repeated and expanded by James (probably Jesus' brother, who was the elder of the church in Jerusalem) in his epistle by that name. "And let endurance have its full [*teleion*] effect, so that you may be mature [*teleioi*] and complete, lacking in nothing" (Jas 1:4). Here, *teleios* is further defined by the word translated "complete," *holokleroi.* This word means "with integrity, whole, complete, undamaged, intact, blameless."[26] Jesus wanted his followers—including women—to be mature, to have integrity, and to be whole people. Both his teachings and his example of treating women as whole people reflected this desire.

Questions for Reflection

1. Why is it that usually women cook and serve meals, especially at church gatherings, but often only males are allowed to prepare and serve the Lord's Supper?
2. Who in today's churches are the ones who usually minister in the sense of being servants?
3. Has anyone in your church ever suggested that the women members leave their food preparations to learn theology at Jesus' feet?
4. What can your church do to take more seriously Jesus' model of a family of equals?
5. What characteristics of Jesus would be considered feminine? Why is this significant for women?
6. How does the second interpretation of the parable of the leavened bread in Luke 13:21 tie in with verses 22-30?
7. When you read Luke 15:3-7 and 8-10, whom did you identify with God: the shepherd, or the woman, or both? Did you find it easier to identify the shepherd as God, and more difficult to identify the woman as God? If so, why?
8. When you read Matthew 13:31-33 and Luke 13:18-21, whom did you identify with God: the man sowing seeds, or the bakerwoman, or both? Did you find it easier to identify the man as God, and more difficult to identify the woman as God? If so, why?

Notes

[1]Elisabeth Moltmann-Wendel and Jürgen Moltmann, *Humanity in God* (New York: The Pilgrim Press, 1983) 43-47.

[2]Elisabeth Schüssler Fiorenza, *In Memory of Her* (New York: The Crossroad Publishing Co., Inc., 1983) 323.

[3]Ibid., 128.

[4]Rachel Conrad Wahlberg, *Jesus and the Freed Woman* (New York: Paulist Press, 1978) 90-96.

[5]Walter Bauer, *A Greek-English Lexicon of the New Testament and Other Early Christian Literature,* 2nd ed. (Chicago: University of Chicago Press, 1979) 437.

[6]Sandra M. Schneiders, *Women and the Word* (Mahwah NJ: Paulist Press, 1986) 11-12.

[7]Fiorenza, 263.

[8]Rosemary Radford Ruether, *Sexism and God-Talk* (Boston: Beacon Press, 1983) 136.

[9]Fiorenza, 147-48.

[10]Schneiders, 48.

[11]Fiorenza, 148.

[12]Ibid., 151.

[13]Schneiders, 47.

[14]Ruether, 64.

[15]Gilbert Bilezikian, *Beyond Sex Roles: A Guide for the Study of Female Roles in the Bible* (Grand Rapids: Baker Book House, 1985) 232, note 3.

[16]Joan Morris, *Against Nature and God* (London: Mowbrays, 1973) 115.

[17]Uta Ranke-Heinemann, *Eunuchs for the Kingdom of Heaven* (New York: Doubleday, 1990) 35.

[18]Leonard Swidler, *Biblical Affirmations of Woman* (Philadelphia: Westminster Press, 1979) 165.

[19]Elisabeth Schüssler Fiorenza, *But She Said* (Boston: Beacon Press, 1992) 215.

[20]Allen C. Myers, *The Eerdmans Bible Dictionary,* rev. ed. (Grand Rapids: Wm. B. Eerdmans Publishing Co., 1987) 648.

[21]Paul J. Achtemeier, ed., *Harper's Bible Dictionary* (San Francisco: Harper & Row, 1985) 552-53.

[22]Swidler, 170.

[23]Ibid., 171.

[24]Moltmann, 117.

[25]Bauer, 809.

[26]Ibid., 564.

Chapter 5

Women Leaders in the New Testament

Most likely there once was a woman pope in the Catholic Church. She was pope from 853 to 855 A.D., calling herself Pope John. She managed to obtain the papacy by masquerading as a man, since this was a time in history when people wore large, concealing robes.

During the thirteenth century, Martin of Troppau wrote about her when he was asked by Pope Clement IV to compile a history of the popes and emperors. Martin reports that Joan studied in Athens and was without equal in her education. She discipled great Christians in Rome and was unanimously elected pope.

Unfortunately, she got pregnant. As she went on a religious procession through Rome, from St. Peter's to the Lateran, she went into labor and gave birth. She delivered between the Coliseum and St. Clement's Church, and in future papal processions that pathway was avoided. It has been said she and the child were murdered on the spot.

A marble statue of a woman and child stood on that street until it was reportedly removed in the sixteenth century to the Vatican Museum. It was then altered to resemble a man. The statue, surprisingly, was never considered one of the Virgin Mary and Jesus.

Another bit of evidence for the existence of a female pope was the use, starting in 1099 A.D., of a chair with a hole in it that the pope-elect had to sit on, wearing a special girdle. It was probably used to make sure the pope-elect was male.

Several other authors mention Pope Joan even before Martin of Troppau wrote his chronicle. This is especially noteworthy, considering the embarrassment her situation caused the Catholic Church. Opposition to the historicity of a woman pope did not even start until the fifteenth century.[1]

Whether or not Pope Joan was aware of it, she had many models for women in leadership in the New Testament. These women headed churches in their homes, served as apostles, prophesied, taught theology, and administered the Lord's Supper as deacons and leaders.

These women exercised the spiritual gifts mentioned in Romans 12:3-8, 1 Corinthians 12:27-28, and Ephesians 4:8. These passages give no indication that the gifts were for men only. For instance, in Ephesians 4:8, the word commonly translated "men" is *anthropois,* a Greek word for humanity, not just for males. God is, after all, impartial toward humans (Acts 10:34).

These spiritual gifts and leadership roles followed the Old Testament pattern of ministry of the word, not of the priesthood. The priesthood involved animal sacrifices and hierarchies, but the model set by Jesus and followed in the early church placed emphasis on servanthood. Jesus provided the basis for this pattern through his example as the suffering servant. There was no use of power structures or hierarchies in his ministry.

The New Testament bears witness to women who followed Jesus' example of leading through serving, thereby exercising their spiritual gifts. There are several such women, although references to them are fleeting and are often obscured by our modern English translations. Fortunately, the Greek text, the language much of the New Testament was written in, has preserved some evidence of their existence, enough information to form a relatively clear picture of the importance these women played in the earliest Christian churches.

Phoebe, a Deacon and Leader

One such hidden leader was Phoebe. She is mentioned only in Romams 16:1-2, and in most modern translations she is simply called a "servant" and a "helper." Such translations do not do justice to the important role Phoebe played in the early church.

Many scholars believe the apostle Paul entrusted Phoebe with carrying his letter from her home church in Cenchreae, a seaport east of Corinth, to the Christians in Rome.[2] An individual with little experience or authority in the church would hardly have made a good candidate for this huge and difficult responsibility. First, the journey from Corinth to Rome would have been long and extremely treacherous and dangerous. A journey by sea invited possible shipwreck; travel by land would have left her open to being robbed and murdered and—in the case of a woman—raped. Second, Paul apparently also believed Phoebe was qualified to answer any questions the Roman Christians might have about the letter's contents. This meant Phoebe had to be a well-educated and experienced theologian. It also appears Phoebe was entrusted with a specific ministry, because Paul asked the Roman Christians to assist her when she needed help. All this paints a picture of a woman who was self-secure, independent, strong, decisive, and determined.

Paul wanted to make sure the Romans were aware of her status and ability to carry out his request by giving her two titles, *diakonon* and *prostatis.*

Diakonon, in most English versions, is translated "servant" when referring to Phoebe. This is a perfectly legitimate translation of *diakonos.* When *diakonos* is used in reference to males in other New Testament passages, however, most modern versions translate it as "minister." There is no textual reason for the males to be called ministers while Phoebe, a woman, is called a servant.

Both within the New Testament and in sources outside the Bible, the word *diakonos* refers to preaching activity. Paul called himself a *diakonos* and described his task as preaching and proclaiming the word of God. Both Paul and Apollos were preachers and teachers, calling themselves *diakonia.* Timothy was asked to fulfill his position as a *diakonos* by enduring hardship and evangelizing, as well as preaching and teaching. Stephen, one of the first seven deacons selected in Acts 6, performed signs and wonders and preached in the Spirit, enough to be martyred for his words (Acts 6:5-60). A table servant would hardly have been a good candidate for such rage and for a stoning. Philip, another of the original deacons, went to Samaria to preach, evangelize, heal, and found communities of faith (Acts 6:5, 8:5-40). It is entirely possible, then, to consider that Phoebe, as a *diakonos,* preached, taught, and evangelized, just as her *diakonoi* brothers in Christ did.

As a *diakonos,* Phoebe had the stamp of approval not only of Paul, but also of God, because the *diakonoi* were gifted with God's grace. Eventually, as the church began forming an official clergy during the first two centuries after Christ, someone called a *diakonos* held a church office along with the authority to preach and teach. Also, according to the *Didache,* an early church document, *diakonoi,* from which we get the word "deacons," assisted with the Eucharistic meal.[3]

We also should not overlook the fact that the early church used terms indicating servitude when referring to those who held authority in the church. They were given the official capacity to perform services for the benefit of the community. For deacons, this could have included table service and seeing to the welfare of widows.

The passage in 1 Timothy 3 refers to male deacons and probably also to women deacons. John Chrysostom, bishop of Constantinople during the fourth century and considered the greatest preacher in the early church, believed it did.[4] The phrase "husband of one wife" was probably necessary to include for the male members of the congregation, because there may have been men in the church who had more than one wife.[5] Although most of the men were monogamous at that time, it was still legal for a man to have more than one wife. Women, however, did not have the option of having more than one husband, so it was not necessary for Paul to write, "the wife of one husband" when referring to women deacons.[6]

Along with being a *diakonos*, Paul referred to Phoebe with the Greek noun *prostatis,* a word used nowhere else in the New Testament. To discover this word's meaning, scholars have studied passages within the Bible using the verb form of *prostatis,* and have researched sources outside of the Bible where the noun form was used. Within the New Testament, the verb form of *prostatis* referred to leading, having charge over others, the ruling activity of elders, and managing households (1 Thess 5:12; 1 Tim 3:4, 5; 5:17).

Some writings outside of the Bible used the noun form of *prostatis* to indicate someone who was a leading officer in a religious organization, a ruler, a leader, or a protector.[7] Classical Greek writings used the masculine form of the noun to indicate a president, chief, patron, or champion.[8] The early church fathers used the masculine noun form for those who presided at the Eucharist and for Christ.[9]

In Romans 16:1-2, the verb used to describe Phoebe was written in the passive form, indicating something being made or being done to another. Mirroring Paul's experience in Colossians 1:23 and Ephesians 3:7, Phoebe was made into a *prostatis*—she did not choose this station for herself.[10] Either a person or a group of people believed in Phoebe and her God-given gifts, and wanted her to carry out the role of *prostatis* for her congregation.

These word studies provide strong evidence that Phoebe was a leader and decision maker for her congregation, possibly as a preacher, a teacher, and a presider over the Eucharist—roles chosen for her and obviously approved by Paul. Paul even said at the end of verse 2 that she was a *prostatis* to him as well; apparently at some point he had submitted to her Christian leadership.[11]

It appears there is a major contradiction between the role Paul approved for a woman in this church and modern translations of letters Paul wrote to congregations. In those letters, it appears he is telling women not to speak in church or to teach or to have authority over men. This is especially true of the letters Paul wrote to the churches in Corinth and Ephesus. These Pauline letters and their relation to women will be discussed in later chapters.

Junia, an Apostle

Paul not only lists the two main qualifications of Phoebe's ministry and authority in Romans 16; he also mentions the qualifications for another woman's important ministry in the early church. The apostle Junia is mentioned only in passing in verse 7. Her brief moment in history provided another testimony to authoritative positions held by women in the early church.

Although she is not mentioned among the original twelve apostles, all of whom were Galilean Jewish males, she may well have been among other apostles mentioned in the New Testament. According to Luke 10, Jesus sent out seventy disciples. Disciples became apostles after Christ's resurrection.

Others became apostles after the resurrection of Christ. The most famous example is Paul, who persecuted Christians until he had a direct experience with Christ on the road to Damascus. Apostles were literally those sent forth with orders from Christ. As apostles, both Andronicus and Junia carried the same authority among the Roman Christians as Paul did for the Christians in Asia Minor.

The only female directly called an apostle in the New Testament was greeted by Paul in his letter to the Romans: "Greet Andronicus and Junia, my relatives who were in prison with me; they are prominent among the apostles, and they were in Christ before I was" (Rom 16:7). It's hard enough to spot this woman apostle unless one knows Greek names; it's even harder with modern translations, many of which turned Junia into a male named Junias. Until the twelfth century, Junia was understood to be a woman.[12] During the thirteenth century, translators toyed with the idea that perhaps this apostle was a male. Unfortunately, their interpretation gained widespread appeal and was concretized in the text during the ensuing centuries. Such an interpretation has little, if any, scholarly backing. There is only a very remote possibility this apostle was a man. No examples have been found in ancient literature of any male named Junias.[13] However, there are more than 250 examples of women named Junia; it was a common Latin woman's name.[14]

Additional evidence for Junia being a female apostle comes from several of the early church fathers. John Chrysostom provides a vivid example. In his commentary on Romans, he was quoted as saying, "Oh, how great is the devotion of this woman, that she should be even counted worthy of the appellation of apostle."[15]

It is entirely possible that there were husband-wife apostolic teams in the early church, especially considering what Paul said in 1 Corinthians 9:5: "Do we not have the right to be accompanied by a believing wife, as do the other apostles?" Husband-wife teams participated in other professions, such as tentmaking (Aquila and Priscilla) and as physicians. These couples had to be teams because in Palestine, a woman could not appear in public and speak without it appearing scandalous. Society greatly restricted women from practicing any sort of profession in the public arena. Wives of apostles would have remained invisible unless the women also were actively involved in ministry. According to Clement of Alexandria, these believing sisters did their ministry in the women's quarters so as not to arouse suspicion among those they approached with the gospel.[16] It is noteworthy that Junia was not described as a wife but only as an apostle.

Some have concluded that if this were a husband-wife team, they were not truly apostles. Sometimes the verse is translated "well-known by the apostles." This is an incorrect English translation of the Greek text, however. The preposition used in the text is *en,* which is translated "within" or "among." The woman Junia was not only one among the apostles, but she also was considered an outstanding apostle.

As if to support his claim that Junia was an outstanding apostle, Paul explained that Junia held the hallmarks of a true apostle—withstanding suffering and hardship. Both Andronicus and Junia had suffered imprisonment for the cause of Christ. This couple must have had a powerful ministry, with Junia certainly doing her part to be imprisoned just as her husband was.

Their imprisonment most likely was due to their apostolic activities and responsibilities. Their job description included teaching, preaching, and doing evangelism. Apostles founded churches and selected their governing bodies. They, along with the prophets, laid the foundation for building Christ's church.[17] Paul encouraged Christians to support apostles and prophets financially, just as the Jewish community supported Jewish priests.

Prophets

Just as apostles laid the foundation for Christ's church, so did the prophets. In the early church, prophets had the same roles and rights as the Old Testament high priests.[18] Prophets commissioned individuals for specific ministries (Acts 13:1-3) and presided at the Eucharist.[19]

Joel's prophecy that women would be prophets was fulfilled by Anna (Luke 2:36-38) and the four daughters of Philip the Evangelist (Acts 21:9). According to Eusebius, a fourth-century bishop, these four daughters were responsible for much of the evangelization of Asia.[20] It is apparent from 1 Corinthians 11:5 that women were openly prophesying in church, and Paul did not tell them to stop. When Paul mentioned prophecy as one of the gifts of the Spirit, he never limited this gift to men.

New Testament prophets held a higher authority in interpreting scripture than did teachers. The gift of prophecy came with the attendant responsibilities of preaching and teaching.[21] The purpose of prophecy was for edification, exhortation, consolation, conviction, and accountability (1 Cor 14:3).

Priscilla, a Theological Educator

Although the gift of prophecy carried more authority than teaching, teachers still provided a very important ministry in the early church. One highly significant woman teacher in the New Testament was Priscilla (Paul called her "Prisca"). She and her husband, Aquila, formed a team that had a major impact on the early church—enough for Paul to recognize publicly that they risked their lives for him and that all the churches of the Gentiles owed them thanks (Rom 16:4).

The couple was unusual because Priscilla, the wife, held the more prominent role of the two. This is apparent from what scholars consider the most reliable sources for the New Testament. In them, Priscilla is named first four of the six times the couple is mentioned. Mentioning the wife first was almost taboo in the ancient world, even an insult to the male, unless the woman was recognized as significantly more important than the husband.

Luke provided a revealing account of Priscilla and Aquila in Acts 18. Paul met the couple in Corinth, and together they traveled to Ephesus. After Paul left town, an Alexandrian named Apollos arrived, preaching the baptism of John. Considered mighty in the scriptures, Apollos would later become a man whom Paul considered his equal in carrying out the gospel. When Priscilla and Aquila heard Apollos preaching, they pulled him aside to teach him "the Way of God more accurately" (Acts 18:26). The verb used for explaining theology in this passage is the same word used to describe how Peter defended himself against members of the circumcision party, and how Paul explained the gospel to the Roman Jews.[22]

It was most certainly Priscilla who took the lead role in teaching theology to Apollos, because she was mentioned before Aquila in this passage. This is stunning when one considers that in the Jewish and Greco-Roman cultures of that time, women were frequently forbidden to read in front of males, let alone to teach them.[23] Apparently, Priscilla had the approval of God, her church, and Apollos to teach theology to a male. Tertullian, a second-century Christian writer and apologist, wrote that "by the holy Prisca the gospel is preached." John Chrysostom called her a teacher of teachers.[24] Other ancient sources also cite the ministry of Priscilla.

Paul's Co-Workers

Priscilla's ministry went beyond teaching. Paul felt great respect for Priscilla. He addressed her before her husband in his greeting (Rom 16:3). He called both her and her husband fellow workers (*synergos*) in Christ. Paul also used the term *synergos* when referring to Timothy and Titus, who were preachers and teachers. The word *sunergon,* "co-worker," derives from two words that form the phrase "to work together." Paul used *sunergon* to indicate his colleagues who were doing similar work. Along with Priscilla, Paul mentioned three other women co-workers: Euodia, Syntyche, and Stephana.

Euodia and Syntyche were named in Philippians 4:3 as Paul's co-workers who shared with him in contending—like athletes—to spread the gospel. Apparently they shared in the same type of work as Paul, Clement, and the rest of Paul's co-workers, which included teaching, preaching, and proclamation of the gospel. Paul made no distinction among the co-workers and gave no hierarchy according to ability or sex. He treated these two women as equals and not as inferior or subordinate people, the same as he treated the male co-workers.

Apparently these women had reached an impasse and were contending with each other. Paul indicated these women held a prominent position in their congregation, because their disagreement created enough of a problem for Paul to mention it personally in his letter. Yet in mentioning it, he respected their right to express themselves and their ability to resolve their own issues. Rather than tell these women to be silent, he asked others in the congregation to assist them in resolving their conflict. He respected these women enough to urge them to resolve their own problem, never taking the issue out of their hands. He treated them as full persons with rights and responsibilities within their congregation. And, as co-workers, he expected their own congregation to be subject to them (1 Cor 16:15-16).

Church Leaders

Because congregations were to subject themselves to Paul's co-workers, they would be subject to Priscilla as co-worker and also as leader of the congregation that met in her home. Paul wrote that a church met in the house of Priscilla and Aquila (Rom 16:5). Again, Paul mentioned Priscilla first, indicating that she acted as the person most prominent in that congregation.[25]

Because the congregation met in Priscilla's home, it met in her domain, because the home was primarily under the influence and control of women. Because the fledgling churches had no place to meet except in homes, they entered into women's domains, which became the churches' domains.[26]

The home, as the meeting place of the earliest Christians, also became the location where discipleship and teaching took place.[27] Women would have been included in activities in the home church and probably had equal status with the men.

In addition, there is evidence that wealthy pagan women gathered in private homes for their worship celebrations. Many prominent and wealthy women converted to Christianity, and they probably would have followed their own custom of opening their homes—their domains—as places of worship and gathering for the Christians.[28] Besides Priscilla (Rom 16:3-5), numerous other New Testament women had churches in their homes: Lydia (Acts 16), Mary (Acts 12:12), Chloe (1 Cor 1:11), Nympha (Col 4:15), Apphia (Phlm 2), and the Elect Lady (2 John).

Lydia, who was staying in Philippi, was perhaps the first convert to Christianity in Europe. Her profession involved both dying purple fabrics in Thyatira and then selling them, probably in Philippi. Her profession was despised because of the unpleasant smells associated with dyeing the fabrics. Lydia also had no proper name (her name given in the text indicates her place of origin—Lydia), so she had no social standing.[29] As a single head of her household, she was responsible for meeting the physical needs of those who lived with her. That would not have been easy, since her profession was despised and required that she work with her hands.[30] As a God-fearer, she regularly joined with other women to pray outside the city, indicating her desire for community. This desire was transferred to her own home when she converted to Christianity; she urged Paul and Silas to join them.

Paul, by accepting her hospitality, apparently supported Lydia as head of a household and of the new church meeting in her home. Yet Lydia, by asking them to come over, was taking on a great risk. These itinerant preachers were usually unpopular, and she risked her own well-being by inviting them into her home as her guests.[31] In fact, shortly after Lydia's conversion, Paul and Silas angered the locals and were thrown into prison. After they were released, they returned to Lydia's home church before heading to Thessalonica. Their next host, Jason, was dragged before the city authorities and accused of acting contrary to the decrees of Caesar (Acts 17:1-9).

A church probably also met in the home of the woman Nympha. Unfortunately, many translations of Colossians 4:15 have converted Nympha into a man. One of the best witnesses to Nympha as a woman is the *codex Vaticanus.* This fourth-century compilation of scripture is one of the most important Greek uncials relied on for modern translations. (An uncial is a literary work written in a formal handwriting style, and the term is used as a classification system for early manuscripts.) Because scholars generally consider the most difficult or surprising text to be the most accurate,[32] it is wisest to go with the *codex Vaticanus* and understand Nympha as a woman with a church meeting in her house.

Two other women heads of churches are mentioned in the first and last verses of 2 John: "The elder to the elect lady and her children, whom I love in the truth. . . . The children of your elect sister greet you." The Greek title for the chosen lady and her chosen sister is *eclecta kyria.* The masculine form of *kyria* is *kyrios,* translated "lord." *Eclecta kyria/kyrios* was a term occasionally used by Christians to designate someone who was ordained or who was the overseer of a body of believers.[33] Both women in this book, though unnamed, were probably heads of their churches. Theologian Clement of Alexandria (150–215 C.E.) supported this conclusion: he said the letter was written to a particular Babylonian woman.[34]

Some have assumed the letter was addressed to a church rather than to a woman. However, the opening phrase in 2 John is written in the same format as the opening phrase in 3 John: "The elder to the beloved Gaius, whom I love in truth." Gaius was certainly an individual; so, too, the elect lady was probably an individual.

Another reason to believe the letter was written to an individual is provided in verses 4, 5, and 13, where the singular "you" is used when addressing the elect lady. The elect lady was apparently head of this church and was addressed as one in authority.[35] The writer switched to the plural form of "you" when he wrote the body of the letter.

The plural "you" was addressed to the "children." The term "children" was a common expression used at the time to designate a group of disciples.[36] These disciples might well have been the members of these women's congregations. Clement of Alexandria described the congregation members as "virgins."[37]

Elders

James Burtchael, in his book, *From Synagogue to Church,* concludes that because the first Christians were Jews, they probably patterned their own assemblies after the synagogue, a worship community they were already very familiar with. He believes there was probably a group of elders who held the highest authority within individual assemblies.[38]

Initially, the apostles and church founders selected the elders. Later, this responsibility most likely reverted to the individual assemblies. Elders were sometimes called *douloi* (slaves) or *diakonoi* (deacons /servants). They preached, taught, appointed other officers, and sometimes even appointed apostles. The elders of the Ephesian congregation were called *episkopoi,* a word translated as "overseers," and Paul told them to shepherd the flock (Acts 20:17, 28; see also Titus 1:5, 7). Usually the authority of a church was given to the elders as a group rather than to one person.

Women may well have been elders in those congregations. The word used to describe the women in 1 Timothy 5:3 was *presbytidas,* which can be translated either as "older" or "elder." These women may have formed a group of elders, because the author wrote about enrolled widows, and in verse 17 referred to the preaching and teaching of elders; nothing specified whether those elders were male or female. John Chrysostom supported this view, stating that this passage refers to women holding the position of deaconness.[39]

Women presbyters were to be *hieroprepeis,* according to Titus 2:3. Translated "reverent," this word is the closest New Testament reference to a priestly function.[40] These women also were told to teach, and the text does not specify if they were only to teach young women or also to teach the young men and slaves.

Women Doing the Word

It is apparent even from these few references that women held vital roles in the establishment of the earliest churches. Their roles were significant enough for Saul of Tarsus to consider them a serious threat; he hauled women off to prison before he was converted to Christianity (Acts 8:3). They probably led, preached, taught, prophesied, and presided at the Eucharist. Some may have even been elders or heads of their congregations. They took seriously what might well have been their baptismal vows,[41] expressed in Galatians 3:27-28:

> As many of you as were baptized into Christ have clothed yourselves with Christ. There is no longer Jew or Greek, there is no longer slave or free, there is no longer male and female; for all of you are one in Christ Jesus.

The phrase "male and female" directly refers to Genesis 1:27, which specifically states that women also are made equally in the image of God. Jesus reaffirmed this concept in Matthew 19:4. These Christian women leaders, acknowledging their status before God, made their spiritual gifts available for God to use for the kingdom of heaven. Paul approved of and encouraged their work and even told other Christians to submit to them because they were doing the work of the gospel (1 Cor 16:16).

Questions for Reflection

1. Why do you think Paul would have entrusted a woman with carrying his letter to Rome, considering how dangerous such a trip would have been?
2. Why would Paul have wanted a woman, Phoebe, to explain what his letter said and to carry out another ministry in Rome?
3. What kind of ministry must Junia have had to be thrown into prison?
4. When the disciple Tabitha died, other disciples sent two men to fetch Peter in a nearby town. Peter came and raised her from the dead, making Tabitha the only person raised from the dead by an apostle in the New Testament (Acts 9:36-43). Why do you think this is so? What might have made her so invaluable to her congregation?
5. What qualities did Lydia need as a merchant and as head of a household?
6. How do you feel about women in church leadership roles such as deacons, priests, pastors, and elders?
7. What special gifts might women be able to bring to ministry?
8. If your church does not currently have women in leadership roles, do you think it should? Why or why not?
9. Do you have any of the gifts and abilities displayed by these outstanding women of the New Testament? Are you using them to serve God?
10. What price must women in your denomination pay if they believe they are called to ordained ministry?

Notes

[1]Clement Wood, *The Woman Who Was Pope* (New York: W. Faro, Inc., 1931) 13-65.

[2]Richard and Joyce Boldrey, *Chauvinist or Feminist? Paul's View of Women* (Grand Rapids: Baker Book House, 1976) 20.

[3]John N. Collins, *Diakonia: Reinterpreting the Ancient Sources* (New York: Oxford University Press 1990) 238.

[4]Kyriaki Karidoyanes FitzGerald, "The Characteristics and Nature of the Order of the Deaconess," in Thomas Hopko, ed., *Women and the Priesthood* (Crestwood NY: St. Vladimir's Seminary Press, 1983) 78.

[5]Uta Ranke-Heinemann, *Eunuchs for the Kingdom of Heaven* (New York: Doubleday, 1990) 35.

[6]Sheri Adams, *What the Bible Really Says about Women* (Macon GA: Smyth & Helwys Publishing, Inc., 1994) 90.

[7]E. Margaret Howe, *Women and Church Leadership* (Grand Rapids: Zondervan Publishing House, 1982) 33.

[8]Ruth B. Edwards, *The Case for Women's Ministry* (Cambridge: University Press, 1989) 59.

[9]Richard and Catherine Kroeger, *Women Elders . . . Sinners or Servants?* (New York: Council on Women and the Church of the United Presbyterian Church in the USA, 1981) 9-10.

[10]Ibid.

[11]Luise Schottroff, *Let the Oppressed Go Free: Feminist Perspectives on the New Testament* (Louisville KY: John Knox Press, 1993) 37.

[12]Alvin J. Schmidt, *Veiled and Silenced: How Culture Shaped Sexist Theology* (Macon GA: Mercer University Press, 1989) 182.

[13]Roger L. Omanson, "The Role of Women in the New Testament Church," *Review and Expositor* 83, no. 1 (Winter 1986): 17.

[14]James D. G. Dunn, Word Biblical Commentary, Vol. 38B, *Romans 9–16* (Dallas: Word Books, 1988) 894.

[15]Kroeger, 10.

[16]Father Jean Danielou S. J., *The Ministry of Women in the Early Church* (London: The Faith Press, 1961) 8.

[17]James Burtchaell, *From Synagogue to Church* (Cambridge: Cambridge University Press, 1992) 293-94.

[18]Elisabeth Schüssler Fiorenza, *In Memory of Her* (New York: The Crossroad Publishing Co., Inc., 1983) 298.

[19]Elizabeth M. Tetlow, *Women and Ministry in the New Testament* (New York: Paulist Press, 1980) 73.

[20]Fiorenza, *In Memory of Her,* 299.

[21]Boldrey, 21.

[22]Aida Besancon Spencer, *Beyond the Curse: Women Called to Ministry* (Nashville: Thomas Nelson Publishers, 1985) 107.

[23]Schmidt, 178.

[24]Kroeger, 9.

[25]Spencer, 130.

[26]Fiorenza, *In Memory of Her,* 176.

[27]Elizabeth Schüssler Fiorenza, *But She Said* (Boston: Beacon Press, 1992) 168.

[28]Fiorenza, *In Memory of Her,* 177, 248-49; and Sharon Hodgin Gritz, *Paul, Women Teachers, and the Mother Goddess at Ephesus* (Lanham MD: University Press of America, 1991) 80.

[29]Schottroff, 131-32.

[30]Ivoni Richter Reimer, *Women in the Acts of the Apostles: A Feminist Liberation Perspective* (Minneapolis: Fortress Press, 1995) 112.

[31]Schottroff, 133-35.

[32]Fiorenza, *But She Said,* 25.

[33]Joan Morris, *Against Nature and God* (London: Mowbrays, 1973) 2.

[34]Ross S. Kraemer, *Her Share of the Blessings* (New York: Oxford University Press, 1992) 176.

[35]Morris, 2.

[36]Fiorenza, *In Memory of Her,* 248.

[37]Kraemer, 176.

[38]Burtchaell, 309-10, 350.

[39]Thomas Hopko, ed., *Women and the Priesthood* (Crestwood NY: St. Vladimir's Seminary Press, 1983) 78.

[40]Letha Scanzoni and Nancy Hardesty, *All We're Meant to Be* (Waco: Word Books, 1974) 63.

[41]Fiorenza, *In Memory of Her,* 217-18.

Chapter 6

Source and Unity

1 Corinthians 11:3-16

There is strong evidence that a woman named Theodora was a bishop in Rome. Two inscriptions in the Church of St. Praxedis show the title "Episcopa Theodora." *One is a mosaic in a chapel. It depicts the head of a woman who is wearing a veil. The word* "Episcopas" *appears above her head, while the word* "Theodo(ra)" *runs down beside her. Unfortunately, the last two letters of her name were removed at a much later date, and the picture of the woman was tampered with to make it appear that the mosaic depicted a man, Theodo. Bishop Theodora's name and title also appear on a marble inscription on one of the columns in the church. There, her name and title were not tampered with.*[1]

As a bishop, Theodora was head of her congregation in Rome. The issue of head—and headdress—is addressed by Paul in his letter to the congregation in Corinth. Corinth, a harbor town in what is now the southern part of Greece, was a busy commercial center of the ancient world. It also was a significant religious center, featuring a widely known temple of the Greek goddess Aphrodite[2] and a community of worshipers of the Greek god Dionysus. These religions probably had a powerful effect on the local people, and some of the religious practitioners may well have been converted to Christianity. It was these converts who may have caused problems for the Corinthian church that Paul addressed in his letters.

His first letter to the Corinthians largely addressed the excesses of church members, excesses that had their basis in a belief that freedom in Christ meant license to behave in culturally unacceptable ways. Paul referred to their immorality and arrogance (1 Cor 5:1-8) and wrote that they exercised their personal freedoms at the expense of those who were weaker in the faith (chaps. 8–10). Members of the congregation also were creating confusion and chaos by their disorderly conduct (chaps. 11–14).

As a main point or theme in the letter, Paul said, "All things are lawful for me, but not all things are beneficial. All things are lawful for me, but I will not be dominated by anything" (6:12). The Corinthians had the freedom in Christ to do some things, but these things were causing other Christians to stumble, and therefore Paul was critical of their behavior. His reasoning: "To the Jews I became as a Jew, in order to win Jews. To those under the law I became as one under the law (though I myself am not under the law) so that I might win those under the law."

Notice the difference between Paul's approach to the Corinthian church and his letter to the Galatian church. The Galatians were being legalistic, so Paul affirmed their freedom in Christ and allowed them more freedom at the Eucharistic table. For the Corinthians, however, he restricted the table service.

Paul probably had to restrict the behavior of the Corinthians because of the influence the congregation felt from the surrounding religions. The temple of Aphrodite had about a thousand female priestesses who served the goddess through sexual relations with worshipers.[3] Women worshipers of Isis let down their hair during their ceremonies,[4] and Isis had a large following in Corinth.[5] Most of the worshipers of Dionysus, also known as Bacchus, were women. Some of these women were called *maenads* ("mad women") because of their worship practices. Worshipers of Dionysus behaved as though they were mad (see 14:23), let down their hair during worship (11:5), gave ecstatic utterances during their services (14:9), got drunk (11:20), played musical instruments, including cymbals (13:1), and encouraged women to reject motherhood (7:14).[6] Women followers of Dionysus were not self-controlled but rather chaotic in their worship. Even the Romans called for restraint of women who worshiped Dionysus.[7] Origen, an early church father (185?–254? C.E.), wrote that Christians were accused of behaving like worshipers of Dionysus.[8]

In addition, there may have been influences on the Corinthian Christians from the Gnostics. The Gnostics held a wide variety of beliefs, but their basic belief was that one had to have certain knowledge (*gnosis*) to receive salvation. Most Gnostics believed, for example, that physical matter, such as the body (and therefore sexuality), was evil, and that there was little difference between male and female.[9] Gnostics preferred that women not wear head coverings.[10] In contrast, Paul affirmed the goodness of marriage and marital sex (7:4) and pointed out the differences between male and female (chaps. 11, 14).

In Corinth, women worshiped with wildness and excess far more than the men; the men worshiped Zeus and Apollo, gods who required restraint. The women probably were attracted to the wild worship services because of all the restrictions society placed on them, so worship became a form of escape and expression. Christian women may well have been converted from these pagan religions and would have brought with them their understanding of how to worship. Paul addressed these religious excesses among the women in chapters 11 and 14.

Head as Authority

Before addressing issues concerning the Corinthian women in worship, Paul first mentioned the relationships between and among humans and the Godhead: "But I want you to understand that Christ is the head of every man, and the husband is the head of his wife, and God is the head of Christ" (11:3). The traditional interpretation of this passage says that because the man is head of the woman, men are therefore to have authority over women. They would then be following the pattern of God as the highest authority, followed by Christ and then men. Using our current English use of the word "head" to mean authority, this interpretation seems to be accurate; certainly a casual reading would leave one with this understanding of the verse. This interpretation, however, has some serious problems.

(1) If this verse is reciting a chain of command, then why is God's authority mentioned after man's authority? It would be much more logical to start at the top: God is the authority over Christ, Christ is the authority over man, and man is the authority over woman. But the verse does not read this way. The next chapter does contain a hierarchy of sorts, reciting the specific positions of ministry in the church in order (12:28). Because Paul did not write 11:3 in a chronological sequence, but did so in the following chapter, we must assume he was not reciting a chain of command but had something else in mind.

(2) If God is the authority over Christ, this would give a chain of command within the Godhead, making the three members of the Trinity unequal. This idea of a chain of command, known as subordinationist theology (Christ is subordinate to the Creator God), was

declared a heresy during the fourth century.[11] Christ is not subordinate to the Creator God; Christ is equal to the Creator God (see John 10:30; 14:7; Heb 1:3).

(3) Paul uses the singular form for man/husband and woman/wife. If Paul were saying all men were the authorities over all women, then he would not have used the singular form. It seems he was speaking about a specific man and a specific woman.

(4) Christ did not come to set up hierarchies and chains of command. Rather, Christ came to serve and to give his life as a ransom for many. For Paul to establish a chain of command that places half of the human race in a subordinate position to the other half is to miss one of the main points of the gospel.

Head as Source

Fortunately, there is another way to interpret 1 Corinthians 11:3 that makes more sense and is not heretical. It is based on the understanding of what the Greek word *kephale,* translated "head," meant at the time Paul wrote his letter.

Modern research has shown that during the first century *kephale* was rarely, if ever, used to indicate authority. Instead, writers such as Paul used the words *exousia* ("authority"; see Rom 13:1-2) and *archon* ("ruler"; see Rom 13:3) to indicate those who held authority or power. According to what is considered the most complete lexicon in current use,[12] the word *kephale* does not mean authority, first, or leadership.[13] The writers of this lexicon studied the meaning of words used in the Bible and other writings of the same period to determine the exact meanings of the word. It was not until the influence of Latin many years later that the new meaning of authority was added to the word *kephale.* There is evidence for this changed meaning in a few of the writings of the postapostolic church fathers during the last third of the first century.[14]

The word *kephale* meant source long before Aristotle (384–322 B.C.E.) clarified this idea in his writings. Given the total lack of knowledge about basic biology during that time in history, we might better understand Aristotle's almost laughable theory about the male physical head being the source of semen and therefore the source of life. First, Aristotle noted that there was a lubricant or form of moisture at every opening of the human head (saliva, tears, and ear wax). He also noted that the body's most luxuriant hair grew on the head, and concluded that this must also be due to the moisture produced by the head. Through all this visual observation, Aristotle concluded the head must be the source of moisture for the body. He believed that human semen, therefore, was produced in the male's physical head, traveled down his backbone, and exited through his genitals. This made the physical head the source of physical life. We must also understand that at the time, it was believed the woman was a sort of garden in which the man planted his seed[15]; there was no knowledge until as late as the nineteenth century that the woman contributed an ovum that provided the other half of the genetic material for the child that came from the woman's womb.[16]

Earlier philosophers, such as Alcmaeon of Croton (sixth century B.C.E.), believed the brain produced semen.[17] Plato (427–347 B.C.E.), Aristotle's teacher, believed the head, which is well protected by the skull, was the source of semen. He said semen moved down the backbone, which also gave it protection, until it reached the genitals.

In the second century C.E., the philosopher Artemidorus of Ephesus explained that the head is like a parent because it is the source from which one receives life, and the head is the source of life and light for one's body.[18]

In the fifth century C.E., Cyril of Alexandria defined *kephale* as source. Commenting on 1 Corinthians 11:3, this Greek church father wrote that Christ is the *kephale* of man because man was made and brought to birth through Christ. He then said man is the *kephale* of woman because he was her source when she was taken from his flesh. Finally, Cyril wrote that God is the source of Christ.[19]

As late as the ninth century, Photius (820–892 C.E.), a Greek theologian and patriarch of Constantinople, directly referred to God as the head of Christ because God is the progenitor of, procreator of, and of like substance to Christ. Photius then said man is the head of woman because man is progenitor of, procreator of, and of like substance to woman.[20]

It is, therefore, understandable why the word *kephale,* when used in the New Testament, has two primary meanings: a source or derivation, or a physical head. Two related English words would include headwaters (the source for a river) or fountainhead (such as the source for a line of bloodstock).

One early church theologian, Tertullian (160?–230? C.E.), in his writing, "Against Marcion," used the word *kephale* to indicate someone who was an author of something.[21]

If we translate *kephale* to mean source, then the Corinthians passage is not hierarchical but cyclical: Christ is the source of every man; the man is the source of a woman; and God is the source of Christ. In other words, Christ is the source of man because Christ was God's agent in creation (John 1:3) and therefore participated in the creation of *ha-adam*. Man is the source for woman, as in Genesis 2:21-23, where God took the rib, or side, from the earth being and fashioned a female. This interpretation is confirmed in 1 Corinthians 11:8 and 12, which specifically say the woman originated from the man. It also makes sense with Paul's use of the singular noun for man and woman in 1 Corinthians 11:3. Finally, God was the source of Christ when Christ was incarnated in human form (Luke 1:32; John 1:14; 5:26; 2 Cor 1:3) through the woman Mary. This is backed up by 1 Corinthians 11:12, which says all things originate from God. If God is the source of Christ, and Christ is the source of man, and man is the source for woman, and through a woman God is the source of Christ, then God is the ultimate source of all things.

This interpretation of *kephale* as source is further substantiated by its use in Colossians 2:10. "You have come to fullness in him, who is the head of every ruler and authority." What did it mean that Christ was head of every ruler and authority? The answer can be found in Colossians 1:16, which describes the creation activity of Christ, including his creation of rulers and authorities. Now, Paul's use of Christ as "head of" makes sense: Christ is the source of all rulers and authorities.[22]

Verse 3 also makes more sense when one considers that humans are made in the image of God. If the image of God is one of three equal, loving persons, then the image of humans should reflect that equality and love. The members of the Godhead are equal, and God made male and female in the image of God, so they also are made to be equal. Therefore, the emphasis of this verse is on unity, not hierarchy.

Head as Head Coverings and Source

Unity was so important to Paul that he spent a lot of time in the next passage, 11:4-16, outlining specifics on how to maintain unity through at least one practice: what to do with one's head during worship to show respect both for God and for the other worshipers.

Paul wanted the Corinthian Christians to follow the customs of their time regarding the appearance of their physical heads, so they would not offend the Jews, the Greeks, or other Christians (10:32). By following local customs, the Christian faith would be more acceptable to the local population, and Christians would be more likely to win converts to Christianity.

The winning of converts may have been affected by the hairstyles women wore while they were praying and prophesying in church. The issue of head coverings pivots around the word *kephale* in 11:4-16. Here, *kephale* takes on double meanings. While it probably means "source" in verse 3, it moves into meaning both source and a physical head in the following verses.

What church members did with their physical heads affected whether they were considered respectable by those in the surrounding community. In ancient Greece, hairstyles carried great symbolism. Paul wanted the Corinthian Christians to adopt acceptable hairstyles for worship. In addition, because of outside influences to the contrary, Paul wanted the Corinthian Christians to make distinctions between males and females during worship. This could easily be done through the use of culturally acceptable head coverings.

Paul said that men who had head coverings (which might have included long hair; see v. 14) while praying or prophesying disgraced their heads (v. 4). In Greece, it was considered disgraceful for a man to have long hair. This especially applied to worship. In addition, the Greeks believed that while worshiping, a man should remove any head covering to give respect to the divine nature of the god he worshiped. It would be dishonorable for a man to worship Christ without a bare head, because this would signal to others in his culture that he did not believe in the deity of Christ. Here's where the double meaning of *kephale* enters in: Worshiping God while wearing a physical head covering would bring dishonor upon the man's head, or source, who is Christ. He would be shaming the one he represented.[23]

In contrast, for women, long hair bound in a veil was the respectable style in Greece. Women who did not have long hair either shaved their heads as a symbol of grief; or had short hair or loosened hair (Num 5:18) as a punishment for adultery; or were *hetaerae,* or male companions, a class of women in Greek culture who are depicted in art with short, completely exposed hair. The *hetaerae* were more than prostitutes; these educated women also were skilled entertainers.[24] Paul did not want the Christian women mistaken for the *hetaerae,* women in grief, or women who had committed adultery.

Women who let down their long hair in public either did so as a sign of uncleanness (Lev 13:45), or as an invitation for an affair, or as part of the worship of pagan gods. A respectable woman who let down her hair in public was highly vulnerable to immediate divorce with no financial settlement.[25]

While women bound up their hair in public, they removed their veils and let down their hair in their own homes.[26] This may have caused confusion because the Christians (including pagan converts) worshiped in private homes. Women may have felt they should be allowed to let their hair down because they were in a private home or because their previous worship practices had included loose hair. Paul, however, wanted them to follow societal decorum in the worship services, even in the privacy of their own homes, and this included covered heads during worship. Women who did not follow the culturally acceptable style of bound and veiled hair would disgrace the church, leading to a removal of the newfound rights women had during worship. Paul wanted the women to keep their rights, so he asked them to follow the custom of bound hair during worship.

The play on the word "head" comes to full force in 11:7: "For a man ought not to have his head veiled, since he is the image and reflection (*doxa*) of God; but woman is the reflection (*doxa*) of man." Here, Paul is playing on the word "head" as both source and as a physical head. The source, or head, of man is Christ, as Paul wrote in verse 3. Therefore, the full glory of Christ, symbolized by the man's physical head, needs to be uncovered during worship. This idea is reminiscent of the phrase "glory of God in the face of Jesus Christ" that Paul wrote in his second letter to the Corinthians (4:6). A man who covered his physical head would be covering the glory of Christ, who is his source; and this would be unacceptable during the worship of God.

In addition, the Greek word *doxa,* here translated "reflection," also can be translated "likeness" (see 1 Cor 15:49). This would make the verse a reminder of Genesis 1:26-27, where *ha-adam,* described as both male and female, is made in the image and likeness of God. The woman, then, while made in the image and likeness of God, also is made in the likeness of humanity. Likewise, if we understand "man" (*andros*) to be *ha-adam* ("the earth being") of Genesis 2, then the head or source of woman is man (*ha-adam*), symbolized here by the woman's physical head. As the reflection of *ha-adam,* the woman's physical head reveals the glory of humanity. This is why *ha-adam,* who became a sexual male in Genesis 2:23, could say, "This is bone of my bone, and flesh of my flesh," in effect seeing himself in the newly formed woman. So the woman is the glory of God's creation, and her head is symbolic of humanity. It also is useful to recall here that in Genesis 1:26-27, woman was made in the image of God, not in the image of a male. Paul never said that woman is not also made in the image of God. Therefore, if the term "reflection" (*doxa*) refers to something that honors or reveals another, then the woman's head, which reveals and honors humanity, must be covered so that she, too, can reflect the glory of God.

Paul clarified the idea of the source or head of woman, saying that the woman originates from man (*ha-adam,* the earth being) and is created to be a companion suitable for the male (vv. 8-9). This is not saying that woman is inferior to or subordinate to man. After all, Paul was fully supportive of women who prayed and prophesied in church, and the authority of the prophet was second only to that of the apostle in the church (12:28).

Paul further discussed and clarified the idea of the origination of men and women (vv. 11-12). Because *ha-adam* is the source for woman, and the woman's physical head is symbolic of humanity, Paul concluded that a woman should have authority on her head because of the angels (v. 10). The Greek text does not say anyone has authority *over* the woman. If Paul had meant that a woman was to wear the veil as a symbol of the authority of a man (probably her husband) over her, he would have written, "Therefore a woman ought to have a symbol of subjection on her head." The verse does not say this.

In fact, the words "symbol of" do not appear in the Greek text. Paul used the phrase *eichen exousian* ("to have power") in this verse, and this phrase always refers to one's personal ability to exercise power (see 1 Cor 7:37; 15:24; 2 Cor 10:8; 13:10).[27] By arranging or covering her head, the woman exercised her own authority to pray and prophesy, just as a queen would wear a crown to display her authority. This authority was new for women of Jewish heritage in Corinth. Unaccustomed to exercising their voice in public worship,[28] these Jewish converts could now pray openly and prophesy during church services. Each woman's new power and authority, given by God and accepted by the church, were displayed like a crown by the use of a covered head. Yet in the eyes of God, both male and female, with unveiled faces, behold the glory of the Lord as in a mirror (2 Cor 3:18).

There was yet another reason for the head covering for women. If the women had worshiped with their heads uncovered, the Corinthian Christian community would have interpreted that as women reflecting the glory of men rather than of God. This would have led to shame rather than deepening the worship experience of the Christians.

The women would have invited more societal disgrace upon themselves and would have distracted the congregation from the worship of God for another reason. In both Jewish and Greek thought, a woman's hair was considered a sexual enticement and so should be kept bound up and under veils.[29] In the view of society, for a woman in ancient Corinth to go into church with unbound hair would probably have been equivalent to a woman today going to worship in a skimpy bikini. Paul's guidelines acted as a means for helping women follow societal decorum by not flinging their hair (specifically, their sexuality) about as pagan women did during the worship of Dionysus and Isis.[30]

The angels mentioned in the verse could be the deliverers of God's messages to the prophets.[31] Or, the verse could refer to the participation of angels in God's worship. When the angels are in the presence of God, they cover themselves (Isa 6:2), so the reference may be for women to cover themselves in worship out of reverence for God because their physical heads symbolize all of humanity. The glory of God is to be revered during worship, not the glory of humanity.

In verses 11 and 12, Paul returns to the idea of the origination of men and women. Qualifying verses 8-9, Paul emphasizes there is to be no chain of command or hierarchy among Christians; they are mutually interdependent. First, he explains that in the Lord, men and women are not independent from each other. According to one researcher, the word *choris* should be translated "different," so the verse would read, "Neither is woman different from man, nor is man different from woman."[32] This affirms what Paul wrote to the Galatian Christians, that "there is no longer male and female, for all of you are one in Christ Jesus" (Gal 3:28).

In verse 12, Paul explains why men and women are dependent on each other: they originate from each other. The only way a woman can originate from a man is through the creation of woman from *ha-adam*, the earth being. This indicates that male and female interdependence and equality have been the will of God from the foundation of the world. Yet, men also are dependent on women, for without women giving birth, there would be no men. Even with this interdependence, both women and men originate from God, sort of a restatement of verse 3.

In verses 13-15, Paul moves away from a theological argument to calling upon the reasoning abilities of the Corinthians, saying it is natural for a woman to have long hair and a man to have short hair. Here, he is probably appealing to what was considered natural among those living in Corinth, following their cultural ideas of respectability in hairstyles. He also may have been affirming the idea that women could keep their long hair and did not have to become like men to be accepted by God, as later Gnostic ideas would teach.[33] In verse 16, he explains that following the hairstyle customs of the times was standard practice for all Christian churches.

Questions for Reflection

1. How does 1 Corinthians 7:1-5 address the concept of mutual submission and mutual equality between husband and wife?
2. What have you been taught about men being the head of women? How did that make you feel?
3. How do you feel about this other interpretation of head as "source"? Does it change anything for you?
4. Where do you draw the line between freedom in Christ and arrogance?
5. Do you practice any personal excesses in your exercise of freedom in Christ that might be a hindrance to another Christian?
6. Are there any cultural influences on your congregation that you consider unhealthy or possibly a hindrance to worship? Is there anyone with whom you can discuss this?

7. Are there any ways your congregation can focus more on glorifying Christ rather than on glorifying humanity during worship services?

Notes

[1]Joan Morris, *Against Nature and God* (London: Mowbrays, 1973) 4-6.

[2]Letha Scanzoni and Nancy Hardesty, *All We're Meant to Be* (Waco: Word Books, 1974) 64.

[3]Patricia Gundry, *Woman Be Free!* (Grand Rapids: Zondervan Publishing House, 1977) 66.

[4]Mary Hayter, *The New Eve in Christ* (Grand Rapids: Wm. B Eerdmans Publishing Co., 1987) 125.

[5]Elisabeth Schüssler Fiorenza, *In Memory of Her* (New York: The Crossroad Publishing Co., Inc., 1983) 227-28.

[6]Richard and Catherine Clark Kroeger, "Pandemonium and Silence at Corinth," *The Reformed Journal* (June 1978): 6-7, 42, 68.

[7]Ibid., 9.

[8]Ibid., 9-10.

[9]R. Gryson, *The Ministry of Women in the Early Church* (Collegeville MN: Liturgical Press, St. John's Abbey, 1976) 5.

[10]Gundry, 67.

[11]Gilbert Bilezikian, *Beyond Sex Roles: A Guide for the Study of Female Roles in the Bible* (Grand Rapids: Baker Book House, 1985) 240-41.

[12]Berkeley and Alvera Mickelsen, "What Does *Kephale* Mean in the New Testament?" *Women, Authority, & the Bible* (Downers Grove IL: InterVarsity Press, 1986) 98.

[13]Ruth A. Tucker, a response to "What Does *Kephale* Mean in the New Testament?" in *Women, Authority, & the Bible,* 118.

[14]Bilezikian, 240.

[15]C. C. Kroeger, "The Classical Concept of 'Head' as Source," Appendix 3, in *Equal to Serve: Women and Men in the Church and Home,* ed. Gretchen Gaebelein Hull (Tappan NJ: Fleming H. Revell, 1987) 270.

[16]Carol Delaney, "The Legacy of Abraham," in *Anti-Covenant: Counter-Reading Women's Lives in the Hebrew Bible,* Mieke Bal, ed. (Sheffield, England: The Almond Press, Sheffield Academic Press, Ltd., 1989) 38.

[17]Kroeger, 270.

[18]Ibid., 271.

[19]Ibid., 277.

[20]Ibid., 278-79.

[21]Tucker, in *Women, Authority, & the Bible,* 113.

[22]Bilezikian, 254-55. In some translations, Colossians 2:10 says Christ is head over all rule and authority. It seems to make sense that Paul would

have used the phrase "head over," considering verse 15, which says Christ disarmed the rulers and authorities. In verse 10, however, Paul did not use the phrase "head over." Instead, the Greek words should literally be translated, "head of." The Greek grammar uses the genitive case, which means the word *kephale* was written as a possessive. The only accurate way to translate the word as a possessive is, "head of."

[23]Gundry, 67.

[24]Ibid., 65.

[25]Paul Jewett, *Man as Male and Female* (Grand Rapids: Wm. B. Eerdmans Publishing Co., 1975) 53.

[26]Scanzoni and Hardesty, 65.

[27]Richard and Joyce Boldrey, *Chauvinist or Feminist? Paul's View of Women* (Grand Rapids: Baker Book House, 1976) 38.

[28]Alvin J. Schmidt, *Veiled and Silenced: How Culture Shaped Sexist Theology* (Macon GA: Mercer University Press, 1989) 147.

[29]Craig S. Keener, *Paul, Women, and Wives* (Peabody MA: Hendrickson Publishers, Inc., 1992) 29.

[30]Sharon Hodgin Gritz, *Paul, Women Teachers, and the Mother Goddess at Ephesus* (Lanham MD: University Press of America, 1991) 85-86.

[31]Fiorenza, 228; and Scanzoni and Hardesty, 66.

[32]Hayter, 229-30.

[33]Ibid., 125.

Chapter 7

Quieting the Tumult

1 Corinthians 14:34-36

In Canon 20 of the Council of Tours, a woman bishop named Terni is mentioned. In a manuscript in the Vatican Library in Rome, there is listed the epitaph "(Hono)rabilis femina episcopa." *This inscription, then, provides another example of a woman bishop.*[1] *The woman Leta was a priest in fifth-century Tropea, a small town in Italy, according to an epitaph on her tomb.*[2]

"Women should be silent in the churches. For they are not permitted to speak, but should be subordinate, as the law also says. If there is anything they desire to know, let them ask their husbands at home. For it is shameful for a woman to speak in church. Or did the word of God originate with you? Or are you the only ones it has reached?" (1 Cor 14:34-36)

Here we have examples of women bishops in early churches, followed by Paul's seeming prohibition against women even speaking during worship services. How did these women bishops, who held such positions of leadership in churches, get around Paul's seeming rule of silence in church? How could Paul condone the praying and prophesying of women in the Corinthian congregation during worship services (1 Cor 11:5), and then in the same letter tell women they must keep silent during worship (14:34-35)? Surely Paul could not have contradicted himself so glaringly in the same letter.

In 1 Corinthians 14, we find the prohibition against women speaking sandwiched between Paul's open statements about his goal for the Corinthian congregation: "What should be done then, my friends? When you come together, each one has a hymn, a lesson, a revelation, a tongue, or an interpretation. Let all things be done for building up" (v. 26). "But all things should be done decently and in order" (v. 40).

Obviously, Paul wanted the Corinthian Christians to do all things properly, in an orderly manner, and for the edification of others. He had good reason for wanting this: He was aware of the powerful influences of neighboring religions on the Christian community. Paul already had told the Corinthians not to exercise pagan religious rites in their worship of the one true God. He wanted to prevent the appearance of madness, as occurred during pagan women's worship of Dionysus. The last thing Paul wanted was for those outside the church to wander by, hear the tumult inside the house, and think those inside were involved in wild pagan worship practices. He wanted the voices raised in worship to edify all those present (see v. 12). This goal could not be reached, however, with the raucous noise of a congregation in which everyone was talking at once. There needed to be some silence and order so people could understand what was being prophesied, what was being prayed, and what was being interpreted.

To encourage order in worship, Paul outlined some heavy restraints to curb the personal excesses of some church members. He told those who spoke in tongues without an interpreter to keep silent (*sigato*) (v. 28; see vv. 23, 27). He told those who prophesied to keep silent (*sigato*) until it was their turn to speak (vv. 24, 29-33). And he told women to keep silent (*sigato*) in church and to direct their questions to their husbands while at home (vv. 34-35).

The Gift of Prophecy

Paul called not only for the silence of those prophesying and speaking in tongues, but also for the silence of the women present. But weren't the women also among those prophesying (11:5)? When Paul called for the silence of prophets, he did not single out men or women. The silence applied to both. This means both men and women prophesied during worship. Later Paul mentioned prophecy among the gifts of the Spirit, but he never specified that any of those gifts could be exercised by men only (12:7-11). He also mentioned the gifts of words of wisdom, words of knowledge, tongues, and the interpretation of tongues. These gifts could hardly have been expressed in silence, so Paul was not silencing all women during worship services. Furthermore, he gave no indication of limitation in God's dispensation of spiritual gifts: "To each is given the manifestation of the Spirit for the common good. . . . All these are activated by one and the same Spirit, who allots to each one individually just as the Spirit chooses" (vv. 7,

11). In the Greek, "each one" is in the neuter gender, which is neither masculine nor feminine.

Paul spoke of spiritual gifts elsewhere, but again never specified that any of those gifts were the sole property of men or of women. He said that God appointed apostles, prophets, teachers, those who speak in tongues, and those who interpret (vv. 27-31). He never said that only men could be apostles or prophets, or that any of these gifts were not to be exercised during worship services. In his letter to the Romans, he addressed all the saints (1:7), listing spiritual gifts: prophecy, teaching, and exhortation (12:6-8)—all of which involve speaking. He did not limit these gifts to either men or women, nor when or where they were to be exercised. Paul listed the spiritual gifts to the congregation at Ephesus as well: apostles, prophets, evangelists, pastors, and teachers. He addressed this letter to the saints at Ephesus, and we know this included women and men because he addressed both individually (5:22, 25). Therefore, Paul never specified that only men could be apostles, prophets, evangelists, pastors, or teachers. Rather, he said that gifts are given to all people: "Therefore it is said, 'When he ascended on high he made captivity itself a captive; he gave gifts to his people' " (Eph 4:8). The word commonly translated "men" in this verse is the Greek word *anthropois,* which is a word for humanity, not for males. Paul encouraged all the saints to exercise the gifts God gave them (4:12-13).

The Limits of Speech in Worship

Based on the passages concerning the exercise of gifts, Paul's statement that "women should be silent in the churches" (1 Cor 14:34) could not have been a blanket statement about all women in all worship services at all times. This silencing of women, then, probably referred either to specific women, or to the type of speaking they were doing.

The only way one can narrow down the type of women Paul was referring to is to say they were married women, because they were told to ask their husbands questions at home (v. 35). If Paul were only trying to silence married women, did that mean the single women could speak in church? Why would Paul make such a distinction in favor of single women? And, if this were the case, then could only single women pray and prophesy? Paul never specified that gifts such as prophecy were designated for certain people, either single or married.

His list of the gifts of the Holy Spirit had no limitations; they were gifts for all humanity. That leaves us with the other option: Paul was referring to a specific kind of speaking the women were doing.

The word in these verses for speaking is *laleo. Laleo* is used throughout this chapter to refer both to speaking in tongues and to those speaking a prophecy. Paul emphasized that those speaking in tongues were not speaking something that was clear or understandable (vv. 5-19). They were uttering sounds. The word *laleo* in classical Greek referred to babbling noises or chatter and could also refer to sounds or tones.[3] In Greek religious rituals, people would shout "*alala,*" a sound without meaning. One ancient hymn, written by Aristophanes and used in the worship of the Greek gods Dionysus, Zeus, and Aphrodite, when translated, revealed the ritual sounds "*Allala*" and "*Lalla,*" which were used by worshipers. It is as though the Greeks shouted "*Lala*" as a way of worshiping their gods.[4] If some of these pagan worshipers had converted to Christianity and were worshiping with the Christian congregation in Corinth, then they would have brought their worship practices with them. Since those practices for women included ecstatic shouting, such as "*lalala,*" then they would have felt at home participating through their shouting while the other Christians were speaking in tongues and speaking out of turn. It could have been this ecstatic shouting that Paul was seeking to silence among the Christian women so passersby would not mistake a Christian worship service for a pagan religious ceremony.

An Exaggeration to Make a Point

Another option for interpreting *laleo* is that the speaking of these women referred to questions they had about the worship service. This possibility is evident because Paul referred to women who had a desire to learn; he encouraged them to wait until they got home to ask their questions to their husbands (v. 35). Paul did seem rather harsh here, telling women they could not ask questions during worship services. When we compare this verse to a similar verse in the same letter, however, we find a style of writing that makes verses 34-35 an exaggeration by Paul specifically to make a point.

In chapter 11, verse 34, there is a similar construction to chapter 14, verse 35: "If you are hungry, eat at home, so that when you come together, it will not be for condemnation." Paul was talking about behavior during the Lord's Supper. Apparently, some people were arriving early for the service so they could eat and drink of the Lord's Supper until they were satisfied, which meant there was little or nothing left for late arrivers. It may have been like a church holding a potluck, and all the rich could arrive early and eat all the food, while the poor, who could not get off work any earlier, arrived later and found nothing to eat or drink. Paul seemed to be telling the overeaters not to partake at all in the Lord's Supper, but we know that could not be the case because Jesus said to partake of the Lord's Supper in remembrance of him. So Paul was exaggerating to make his point: Eat at home before you come to church so you won't be tempted to gobble all the food and get drunk, depriving your fellow Christians of their opportunity to partake in the Lord's Supper. Yes, participate in the Lord's Supper, but do it in a manner that is becoming of a Christian. Consider how your behavior affects others in the congregation, and behave in a concerned way toward the others.

Likewise, in 14:34-35, Paul told women that their behavior in church was improper because they were speaking in a way that others found disruptive. He exaggerated by telling them not to speak in church but to remain silent, and if they had questions, to ask them to their husbands when they returned home. Paul was not telling these women they could never speak in church. Paul's point was this: When you are in worship, do not speak disruptively, but be considerate of others. Be quiet and patient until the right time to speak. If you can't speak in a way that edifies other church members, then remain quiet.[5]

Improper Etiquette

As a third possible way to understand Paul, perhaps some men were prophesying, and then some of their wives were passing judgment on, testing, or questioning those prophesies (see vv. 29-33). This probably would have caused the husbands some embarrassment, which would not have left either the wife or the husband edified.

The Greek biographer and philosopher Plutarch (46–120 C.E.) wrote about proper behavior for those attending speeches in the Greco-Roman world. This etiquette most likely would have applied to preaching in churches. According to Plutarch, it was considered rude to ask speakers questions unrelated to their topic, to challenge speakers without having fully understood the topic before issuing the challenge, or to nit-pick at the points speakers made. Plutarch even noted that it was rude to whisper during a lecture.[6]

Members of a congregation most likely to ask questions were the women, because they would not have received much of a religious education, particularly a Christian education, since the faith was new. These women probably had not attended many public lectures and might not have been as aware of proper etiquette when someone was speaking in public. Paul was probably telling the women not to behave in a way considered rude nor to speak disruptively. He wanted them to understand how to behave properly in a Christian worship setting.

The silence Paul referred to could also be the silence of one who listened intently to a teacher: "They listened to me, and waited, and kept silent for my counsel" (Job 29:21). The goal of this silence was to learn, just as the goal of Paul's silencing of the prophesying was so all could learn. Paul wanted the women to learn; he just asked them to learn in silence out of respect and to ask their questions at home.[7]

Silence and Subjection

Paul also asked the women to subject themselves. He was not imposing any male authority figures on the women to keep them silent and subject. Rather, he was asking the women to choose to be silent and to subject themselves. In other words, he wanted the women to exercise more self-control and self-restraint so their behavior would become more edifying, proper, and orderly.

Verse 34 refers to "the law," but no Old Testament law says that women are to subject themselves or be silent during worship. Paul probably was referring to a rabbinical law used in synagogues for Jewish worship and applied to women to promote orderly worship of God. Paul would hardly have been one to lay down the law for women; he was too concerned about freedom in Christ, especially in his letter to the Galatians. Paul was very concerned about order in worship, however, so he likely was asking the women in the Corinthian congregation to follow a Jewish law in order to make the Corinthian worship experience less disruptive so that everyone could learn.

While Paul asked the women to be less disruptive during worship, he also encouraged them to learn whatever they could by asking their husbands. He did not want the women to ask their husbands questions in church that would be embarrassing, so he asked the wives to wait until they were in the privacy of their own homes before asking. Paul's short-range solution to the disruption problem was for women to be silent during worship. His long-range solution was for women to become educated in their faith.

When Paul encouraged women to ask their husbands questions at home, he acknowledged that women want to learn about their faith, that women are intellectually capable of learning,[8] and that women have a right to religious education. He wanted the men to take responsibility for the theological education of their wives. In these three ways, Paul was affirming women's rights to know and to learn, something commonly denied to women in his culture. This made Paul a rather progressive man of his times where women's rights were concerned.

Questioning the Men

Paul's encouragement of female religious education might have been met with resentment, anger, or disbelief on the part of men in their congregations. Paul braced for this kind of response by addressing it head-on: "Or did the word of God originate with you? Or are you the only ones it has reached?" (v. 36). The verse begins with the Greek particle *e,* which can be translated "or," indicating Paul was about to introduce a question, perhaps even a rhetorical one. The words seem to be written with a sarcastic bite, almost as though he was saying, "Who are you men to think that it is only from you that God's word went forth? Who are you men to think that the word of God has come only to you and not to women?" Paul addressed these questions to the men, not to the women, because the second "you" has a masculine adjective in the Greek text. Paul wanted the men in the congregation to understand that the word of God was brought forth by both men and women, and that it came to women as well. Therefore, women had the right to ask questions and to speak the word of God in church, though in an orderly manner. God did not give men a monopoly on the Word of God.

A Call to Order

Paul reemphasized his call for order among the Corinthians: "But all things should be done decently and in order" (v. 40). This verse sums up what Paul expressed throughout chapter 14. His bottom line was not the silencing of women in church, but encouraging the

Corinthians to stop their disruptive behavior. He desired that both women and men act in a way that edified all of the church members and glorified God. Paul made it clear that the principle of love has priority over Christians' rights to freedom.

Questions for Reflection

1. How did the utterance of ecstatic speech of the Dionysus worshipers differ from the tongue speaking of Christians? (see Acts 2:4-11; 1 Cor. 12:10)
2. How does the speaking in tongues described in 1 Corinthians 14 compare to true Christian tongue speaking and that of worshipers in other religions? (see v. 33)
3. What other forms of speech besides those addressed in this chapter might be unedifying to other church members? What can you contribute to curbing such speech?
4. Are there any other forms of excess occurring during your church's services that make it more difficult for others to worship God? What can you contribute to curbing such excesses?
5. Why was order such a high priority for Paul in this letter to the Corinthians?
6. What happens if a woman has spiritual gifts that are not exercised? (see Eph 4:12-16; Rom 12:3-8; 1 Cor 12:26-27)
7. What role does Christian love play in being orderly during worship?

Notes

[1]Joan Morris, *Against Nature and God* (London: Mowbrays, 1973) 6.

[2]Mary Ann Rossi, "Priesthood, Precedent, and Prejudice: On Recovering the Women Priests of Early Christianity, Containing a Translation from the Italian of 'Notes on the Female Priesthood in Antiquity,' by Giorgio Otranto," *Journal of Feminist Studies in Religion* 7, no. 1 (Spring 1991): 86.

[3]Walter Bauer, *A Greek-English Lexicon of the New Testament and Other Early Christian Literature,* 2d ed. (Chicago: University of Chicago Press, 1979) 463.

[4]Richard and Catherine Clark Kroeger, "Pandemonium and Silence at Corinth," *The Reformed Journal* (June 1978): 10.

[5]Craig S. Keener, *Paul, Women, and Wives* (Peabody MA: Hendrickson Publishers, Inc., 1992) 72.

[6]Ibid., 82-83.

[7]Ben Witherington III, *Women in the Earliest Churches* (Cambridge: Cambridge University Press, 1988) 102-104.

[8]Donald G. Bloesch, *Is the Bible Sexist?* (Westchester IL: Crossway Books, 1982) 32.

Chapter 8

Authorization to Teach

1 Timothy 2:11-15

The Acts of Paul and Thecla, part of the New Testament apocryphal literature, tells the story of a woman apostle named Thecla. Shortly before she was to marry, Thecla heard Paul preaching. She became so entranced by the gospel that she chose to follow Paul and remain single. Her devotion led to extensive persecution, but she survived and taught the gospel in the house of Tryphaena. Later, when she told Paul she was returning to Iconium, he ordered her to go and teach the word of God. She did teach there, and later taught in Seleucia until she died.[1] *Thecla was honored as a saint by the Roman Catholic Church until 1969.*[2]

"Let a woman learn in silence with full submission. I permit no woman to teach or to have authority over a man; she is to keep silent. For Adam was formed first, then Eve; and Adam was not deceived, but the woman was deceived and became a transgressor. Yet she will be saved through childbearing, provided they continue in faith and love and holiness, with modesty." (1 Tim 2:11-15)

The woman apostle named Thecla probably was a fictional character, but her story was popular enough among the early Christians to be written in six different languages.[3] Thecla's story, alongside stories of women leaders recorded in the New Testament, modeled and validated the notion that God's Spirit allows women to teach and hold positions of authority in the Christian church.

The 1 Timothy passage seems to contradict the validity of these roles for women. The writer of this letter called himself the apostle Paul, although some scholars dispute this claim. Nevertheless, the letter was one of the pastoral addresses to Timothy, leader of a congregation at Ephesus. Ephesus was a busy harbor town by the

Mediterranean Sea in Asia Minor (what is now Turkey) that strategically linked the East with the West, making it a major center for trade in the Roman Empire.[4]

Because the stream of humanity passing through Ephesus brought many ideas from various parts of the then-known world, the city became a great cultural and religious center. Already, for perhaps more than a thousand years, the great mother goddess had been worshiped in Ephesus.[5]

For hundreds of years, the city was home of the great Artemisian, a temple built to the goddess Artemis around the sixth century B.C.E.[6] The fame of this temple spread, and it became known as one of the seven wonders of the ancient world. It also served as the largest bank in antiquity. It burned down in 356 B.C.E., but was rebuilt and stood until the third century C.E.[7] The worship of Artemis probably affected everyone in Ephesus because of the religion's widespread popularity—the worship involved citywide celebrations, and her places of worship hired numerous employees.[8] The religion brought wealth and power to many.[9]

The mass of people and ideas moving through Ephesus brought plenty of outside influences that probably affected the Christian congregation in Ephesus. Paul's first letter written to Timothy appears to address a specific problem (1 Tim 1:3, 4, 6, 7, 19, 20; 5:13). Apparently some false teachings were circulating among church members, particularly the women, and these ideas were causing problems for the congregation. The situation was probably becoming desperate, because both letters to Timothy seem to cycle through the theme of false teachings (see also 1 Tim 4:1-3; 6:3-5, 20-21; 2 Tim 1:15; 2:16-18; 3:6-9; 4:3-4, 14-15).

In addition to the problems with false teachers, the church at Ephesus probably had both Jewish and pagan converts. Pagan women, generally confined to the home and certainly not educated, had found some measure of freedom through their involvement in religious activities.[10] Naturally, many of them worshiped the mother goddess because it gave them an outlet for expressing themselves as women. To those living in Asia Minor, where the mother goddess held great sway, it was natural for women to lead in worship. In this cult, women were selected as chief priestesses.[11]

By contrast, rabbinic Judaism did not permit women much participation in Jewish worship services. For example, it has been written that ten men had to be present for a synagogue to begin a service. If there were nine men and a thousand women present, a worship service could not begin.[12] Although Jewish synagogues outside of Israel tended to offer women more freedom, they were still quite restrictive toward women in their religious practices.

Bringing together people who had practiced such diverse styles of worship to form the Christian church at Ephesus was bound to lead to problems. These problems probably inspired Paul to write the letter as he did. One problem involved the behavior of women in the congregation and their openness to unorthodox ideas (1 Tim 3:14, 15).

The letter contains only a brief passage about the problems concerning women in the congregation, but these few verses have been used for two millennia to limit the service of women in the Christian community. Currently, it is still used to keep women silent in church or to keep them from teaching males. It also is used as a proof-text to keep women in some denominations from preaching.

If Bible-believing Christians take such an English translation literally, then they will believe that women are to learn quietly, never to teach or have authority over men and, with some translations, bear children in order to be saved. Yet such an interpretation does not square with much of the rest of Scripture, such as the New Testament records of women who preached, taught men, and vocally prophesied in churches—all with God's and Paul's approval. In addition, Christians know that salvation is through grace by faith, not through the bearing of children. Outside of the Bible, history is full of godly women who had no children. With all the biblical and historical evidence to the contrary, the modern translations and interpretations of this passage should probably be more closely scrutinized.

The other problem with this passage is that parts of it are used as proof-texts to prevent women from exercising all of their God-given gifts. One or more of the verses tend to be taken out of context and used indiscriminately, even dogmatically, to "prove" that women are neither to teach nor have any authority over men. There is danger in such a practice because the verses should be read together as well as in their historical and biblical context to be properly interpreted. These verses belong together, as can be seen by the connecting language that exists between the verses. This passage appears to be part of a single idea, a cohesive whole. As such, one must find what those links are and interpret the passage as a single unit. Only then will the passage make sense and the interpretation be legitimate.

Fortunately, modern research, particularly that by Catherine Clark Kroeger, sheds important new light on this passage that assists in the interpretation and understanding of it. Greek manuscripts also offer some flexibility and possible insight, as does research outside the biblical domain. The following interpretation of this passage is actually quite positive for women.

Verse 11

"Let a woman learn in silence with full submission."

The Greek verb *manthaneto,* translated here as "learn in silence," can mean to learn, to find out, or to attend a rabbinic school, as in John 7:15.[13] We can compare the verb *manthano* with the same verb found in Acts 11:18, where the apostles "were silenced" by becoming quiet, glorifying God, and speaking about God. The verb doesn't mean the apostles did not speak; it probably meant they were paying attention to what someone else was saying.

Likewise, Jewish rabbinical students learned by keeping silence. Their silence communicated a spirit of openness to and respect for the teacher and the material being taught.[14] It appears that Paul wanted the Ephesian Christian women to learn as rabbinical students learned—quietly, so they would be receptive to the teachings and would show respect for their teachers.

Paul used a verb tense that implied continuous activity: let a woman continue to quietly receive instruction.[15] This indicated that the women were learning about Christianity on a continuing basis; perhaps they were receiving a thorough grounding in the Christian faith.

To understand the impact and positive nature of this verse for the Ephesian women, consider the widespread customs at the time. Women in the ancient world rarely obtained any kind of education. Jewish women in particular did not receive religious education in the first century. With few exceptions, they were not even taught the Torah, the Jewish books of the law. The sentiment against women receiving any religious education was brought into sharp focus by one rabbi who wrote that it was better to burn the Torah than to teach it to a woman.

Yet Paul encouraged women to learn about their faith in the way rabbinical students learned. The verse shows a radical movement toward the idea that women were full participants within the Christian community and had the intelligence to comprehend the teachings of Jesus. Any interpretation of this verse, even the most detrimental toward women, still reveals Paul's sharp departure from the attitudes of his contemporaries. When it came to learning about the Christian faith, he saw the importance of educating women.

Apparently, Paul realized the need for educating the Ephesian women because of the heresies circulating among members of the congregation. The men had probably already learned the faith basics; now the women needed to learn as well. Without a proper education, the women could not protect themselves against heresies, and might, in fact, have been helping to spread false doctrines. It also is possible the women who were receiving instruction were simply talking unnecessarily, and needed to pay more attention to the teachings so they would learn them accurately.

In verse 11, women are told to learn not only quietly, but also submissively. What would such a statement have meant to the Ephesian women? They probably were familiar with the language idiom of the Near East in which the words "silence" and "submission" were combined as a formula indicating a willingness to follow what they were being taught.[16]

Here, when Paul asked for "silence and submission," he apparently wanted the women to be receptive to the material they were being taught. In this verse, then, submission is a synonym for silence and explains the type of learning women were to take part in.[17] Paul wanted these women to receive a sound biblical education, probably so they would not be hoodwinked by false doctrines.

Verse 12

> "I permit no woman to teach (*didaskein*) or to have authority (*authentein*) over a man; she is to keep silent."

Although our English translations seem to say so, it makes no sense to translate and interpret verse 12 as a directive for women never to teach men. In 2 Timothy 4:19, Paul asks Timothy to greet Prisca and Aquila. Prisca, also called Priscilla, taught theology to Apollos, whom

Paul considered his equal. We know it was Prisca who did the primary teaching because she was mentioned before her husband, Aquila, a significant breach of tradition in the ancient world that indicated her leadership in that relationship. If Paul had a problem with Prisca teaching, he might not have mentioned a greeting to the couple. He certainly would not have mentioned Prisca's name first again because it would have acknowledged her leadership role within the marriage relationship, and this greeting would have encouraged her in that role.

In addition, verse 12 must harmonize with 2 Timothy 2:2: "And what you have heard from me through many witnesses entrust to faithful people (*anthropois*), who will be able to teach others as well." The word *anthropois,* usually translated "men" in this verse, actually is a word for humanity. If Paul wanted to refer to males only, he would have used the Greek words *aner* or *andros.* By using the inclusive *anthropois,* Paul was indicating that the women, who were in the process of getting a theological education, eventually would be expected to teach others as a sign of their faithfulness to God.

Fortunately, there are other ways of interpreting verse 12. Here are a couple of the more positive interpretations. According to one interpretation, the verb "to permit" is written in a tense that implies continuous present action. To more accurately translate, the verse could say, "I am not currently permitting a woman to teach. . . ." The verb is not written in the command mode. The command mode appeared in the previous verse, where Paul was telling women he wanted them to learn. But in verse 12, he was telling them he was not permitting them to teach *at that time,* which implies that those who learned might eventually teach—just not right now.[18]

If we buy this translation, we must ask why Paul would prefer for women to learn as rabbinical students, yet not to teach at that time. Paul was addressing their lack of proper theological education. If we look at Titus 1:10-11, we see the writer wants another group silenced—men who were "idle talkers and deceivers." So it is not a matter of Paul wanting to silence all women in all churches for all time. Rather, Paul wanted to end a particular problem with false teachings, which apparently were captivating women in that church at that time.

Not only were the women in the congregation uneducated, they also were prone to spreading false teachings, as indicated in 2 Timothy 3:6-7: "For among them are those who make their way into households and captivate silly women, overwhelmed by their sins and swayed by all kinds of desires, who are always being instructed and can never arrive at a knowledge of the truth."

Because at least some of the women had been misled into teaching false ideas, Paul needed to bar them from teaching until they learned more orthodox doctrine. In addition, it is possible that the Greek structure of the sentence could be an indirect statement with a redundant negative. According to Greek grammar, then, the focus of the sentence falls on the content of the teachings rather than on the women's ability to teach or on their gender.[19] In the same way, the writer of the book of Hebrews pointed to those who should have been more mature in the faith than they were so they could become teachers. Paul did not limit the teaching function to men, as indicated by his support of Priscilla.

Why would Paul not allow women to have authority at that time? Naturally, if the women were uneducated and were teaching false doctrine, they would have no business holding a position of authority in any church. Rather, Paul insisted that they learn the gospel. Once they became educated, these women could be entrusted with the Christian message and could begin teaching and moving into positions of authority. Paul did not prevent other women from holding positions of authority in the church because we have his writings commending many women in their ministries. It would be too contradictory for him to insist that women in one congregation never teach or have authority over men, while he commended other women for their teaching and authority.

If the Ephesian congregation was having trouble with women teaching false doctrine, then the ready solution would be for them to learn in a rabbinical fashion so they could withstand heresy. Then they would be prepared to teach a purer theology and move into positions of authority.

Yet, there is another way to translate and interpret this verse to bring it into greater harmony with Paul's other teachings and his behavior in the New Testament. The interpretation must also fit into the context of the entire passage. The passage is part of the Pastoral Epistles. Throughout these three books the word for teaching is *didasko*, and it appears in various forms. In these epistles, *didasko* almost always has a modifier connected to it. The modifier indicates the form of teaching being done.[20] To discover the form of the teaching in verse 12, the Greek word *oude* provides the clue. *Oude* appears between *didaskein* ("to teach") and *authentein* ("to have authority"). This could indicate that the two ideas, *didaskein* and *authentein,* are related concepts, since they are joined by *oude.*[21]

Authentein is a Greek verb that appears nowhere else in the entire New Testament. Consequently, there is some question about how to translate it. If Paul had meant simply "authority," as this verse is often translated, he probably would have used the Greek word *exousia* (which is the Greek word that comes closest to meaning "authority" in English) rather than *authentein.* Also, if Paul was only discussing authority, he would be in direct contradiction with his previous writings, such as the authority he vested in Phoebe.

Before the time of Christ, the verb *authentein* had four basic meanings: (1) to be responsible for an action, especially murder; (2) to dominate; (3) to usurp another's rights; and (4) to claim authorship.[22]

Authentein, used in the context of this passage, could suggest one who was domineering or overthrowing authority, possibly to the point of destroying another person.[23] If the verb indicates dominance, one possible translation that ties together the two verbs ("to teach" and "to dominate," connected by *oude*) is that Paul was not allowing a woman to teach dominance over a man. Dominance is an abuse of power, the opposite of the servant model of leadership Jesus demonstrated and taught.

There is another possible translation. According to etymologist Pierre Chantraine, the root word *authentes* (the word from which the Greeks got the word *authentein*) referred to someone who originated something or was responsible for a situation.[24] From this root, *authentes* was used to identify one who ruled or who was responsible for a crime, usually murder.[25] By about the first century, the noun form of *authentes* was used by several writers to indicate an originator or author of something.[26] In this verse, the verb tense of *authentein* indicated possession, a description, or something specific. Applying this information, the verse would read, "I do not allow a woman to teach that she is the author of a man."[27]

It is quite possible that women were teaching such a doctrine in the first century, either as a forerunner to a religious belief system known as Gnosticism or as Gnosticism itself. Gnosticism was a mystery religion that some scholars claim was well developed by the first century C.E.[28] In Gnostic religious systems, members were initiated when they gained a certain type of knowledge (*gnosis*). There were many types of Gnosticism, just as today there are many denominations within Christianity. Some of the Gnostic teachings were pulled from the Old and New Testaments and modified, to the point where some teachings were contradictory.[29] Among those writings were often extensive genealogies, which captured the imagination of some Gnostics. Many of them believed they would achieve salvation if they understood their genealogical origins. Paul argued against this fascination with origins in 1 Timothy 1:4 and Titus 3:9.

Among the theories of origins were Gnostic creation stories that taught Eve was created first, and that she herself created Adam. This idea would certainly hold great appeal in a city where the mother goddess Artemis had such an enormous following. For the women living in Ephesus, Artemis was a fertility goddess and a virgin (at that time, the word "virgin" meant the woman was simply unmarried or unattached).[30] A story showing that Eve was created first would fit quite easily into their belief systems. The Ephesian community provided fertile ground for the spread of such myths. Women would be receptive to such stories and eager to pass them along to others. This is probably why the verse ends with the phrase, "she is to keep silent." If Paul wanted the women to stop teaching false ideas, such as the idea that woman was the author of man, he would have used the word silence, as he does. If he wanted to get across the message that women should never have authority over men, he would have used the word submissive instead. Rather, he wanted the women to quiet down so they could learn sound doctrine.

With this background, it appears Paul was addressing a congregation that had a specific heresy threatening it. Paul used this technique of mentioning a heresy and then arguing against it in several scriptures (see Rom 3:8; 1 Cor 15:12-57; 1 Tim 4:3-5; and 2 Tim 2:17-19). In 1 Timothy 2:12, Paul was probably countering a heresy that included a belief that woman was the author or source of man, because some were teaching that Eve was created first. Paul moved to counter this myth in the following two verses.

He connected verses 11 and 12 to verses 13 and 14 with the Greek word *gar,* signifying that he was about to further address the issues raised in verses 11 and 12. Paul's explanation included the creation account in Genesis to counter false creation story teachings and to verify two important ideas: Woman is not the author of man, and when one is deceived, transgression follows.

Verses 13-14

> "For Adam was formed first, then Eve; and Adam was not deceived, but the woman was deceived and became a transgressor."

It appears, from Paul's need to remind the Ephesians of the Genesis account, that verses 13 and 14 were his response to the myths and strange doctrines that were being spread within Timothy's congregation (1 Tim 1:3-4; 4:7). These tales probably included the Gnostic idea that Eve was created first and that Adam was deceived into believing he was created first, as written in "On the Origin of the World" and "The Hypostasis of the Archons." If Eve was created first, she would have been the source or author of Adam, rather than the other way around.[31] Often, among Gnostics, Eve was considered superior to Adam and even his spiritual teacher, as in "The Apocryphon of John."[32]

Gnostic tales emphasizing the superiority and earlier creation of Eve would have been met with open arms by women in Asia Minor, where the influence of the mother goddess had been so strong for hundreds of years. The Artemis cult at Ephesus taught a doctrine strikingly similar to that of the Gnostics: The mother goddess was created first, before any male gods or consorts, and was a giver of life and of knowledge. Later, according to the myths, her male consort was created.

Storytelling in itself was an important pastime in Asia Minor. It was where Aesop weaved his fables, and where the earliest Greek prose genre, called historiography, was developed.[33] A story about Eve's preexistence would be a direct contradiction to Paul's stated understanding of the second creation account. Paul wanted the focus returned to Genesis 2–3, in which his rabbinical interpretation of events pointed to the creation of Adam first, followed by Eve; and that Eve was the one deceived, an event that led to transgression. It was quite logical for Paul to give the Ephesians the rabbinical interpretation of the second creation account, because he spent years as a rabbinical student under the guidance of the rabbi Gamaliel (Acts 22:3).

As we saw in the chapter on the creation accounts, this interpretation was based more on tradition than on the Hebrew text itself. Paul probably chose to use this traditional interpretation for two reasons. First, the Ephesians were probably only familiar with the rabbinic interpretation of the story, just as most Christians today are only taught the traditional interpretation of the account. Rather than go into a lengthy discussion of what the Hebrew text really said in the original passage, Paul used the traditional understanding to make a related point to the Ephesian Christians.

According to tradition, the male named Adam was created before Eve. It was of great importance for Paul to make this point to the Ephesians because the pagan converts were probably projecting their beliefs about Artemis onto Eve. They probably believed Eve was first in creation, and therefore she was superior to Adam, perhaps even his spiritual teacher; they also would have glorified Eve as the provider of both knowledge and of life, just as they did with Artemis.[34]

Paul probably sought to bring some balance to this view by reminding the congregation that the traditional interpretation of Genesis taught that Adam was created first, not Eve. Paul employed other interpretations of the creation narrative to communicate different messages to other congregations, such as the church in Rome. In Romans 5:12-21, Paul blamed only Adam for the fall, and didn't even mention Eve's part in the event. Obviously Paul wasn't talking out of both sides of his mouth; he was probably looking at the problems he was addressing in specific congregations and choosing biblical examples to drive home either the need for change or a certain truth each congregation needed to hear. Paul used the Scriptures to make specific points to the churches he was writing to, just as a preacher today might draw on certain biblical accounts to make a point in a sermon.

Second, Paul had a specific point to make to the Ephesians, and the traditional interpretation best suited his purposes. If he had appealed to Genesis 1:27 in his argument, that both women and men are made in the image if God, he probably would have only perpetuated the problem. He needed to make an interpretation of the creation account to communicate that deception and false ideas lead to trouble. And it was probably primarily the women in the congregation who were being deceived, so he chose to give an example of a woman being deceived to clarify his point.

Paul wanted to end the spread of false doctrines by Ephesian women. After all, a story showing Eve as the first created human would have appealed more to the women, and they had little or no educational background from which to discern what they were hearing.

So, to communicate the problem better to the women, Paul chose to make an example of another woman—Eve—to offset the problem. Verse 14 provided this counteroffensive. Here, Paul used Eve as an historical example of what happens when someone is deceived into following after a false idea. Eve was deceived by the serpent, which resulted in the fall of all humanity. The women at Ephesus were being deceived by myths, and this would also lead to their downfall if they didn't stop to learn a purer doctrine as rabbinical students.

One of the false myths they probably believed was that Adam was deceived, not Eve, as in "On the Origin of the World." In this story, Adam was put to sleep by higher authorities and then was deceived into believing he was the source of Eve.[35] If such a story were circulating among the Ephesians, Paul would have wanted to set the record straight. He chose to address the problem by pointing out that instead of Adam being deceived by higher authorities, it was Eve who was deceived by the serpent.

Even if such a story were not known by the Ephesians, Paul still found a way to make an example to the women of Ephesus to help them shake off the deception they were living under. So he came right out and said Adam was not the one deceived, but rather Eve was deceived. Elsewhere, he used another female known to all the women as an example of what happens to women when they allow themselves to be deceived.

Paul wasn't picking on Eve and the women of Ephesus because they were female, however. Elsewhere, he used the deception of Eve to illustrate the deception of all believers, both male and female (2 Cor 11:3). So, Paul's focus was on the danger and consequences of deception, not on the gender of those being deceived. Apparently, he didn't see women as being more gullible to false doctrine than men, though in Ephesus women may have been more vulnerable because of their cultural surroundings. In his letter to Timothy, Paul simply wanted to end the spread of myths and false doctrines among the women he was addressing. Apparently, he believed that reminding them of the Hebrew creation account would get their attention.

To end the spread of the myths, Paul's solution was to provide the women with a proper Christian education, under the authority of the Scriptures, so they eventually would be able to share in ministry, which included teaching.

Yet another false idea was being spread among the Ephesian women, and Paul addressed this problem in the next verse.

Verse 15

> "Yet she will be saved through childbearing, provided they continue in faith and love and holiness, with modesty."

Some persons translate verse 15 to mean that women can only receive salvation from sin through giving birth to children, which implies that women who never have children cannot receive salvation. Such an interpretation flies in the face of Paul's teachings about justification by faith, by the grace of God rather than by works (Eph 2:8-9). Fortunately, there are numerous ways of interpreting this verse, and we will look at a few of them.

Some scholars have suggested that the childbearing refers specifically to Mary bearing the child Jesus, since the phrase can be translated, "through *the* childbearing." Because here the word "the" appears with the word "childbearing," it is possible the verse could refer to a specific childbearing event. It could be referring back to verses 13 and 14, and would indicate that the consequences of Eve's sin are not forever. Rather, the promise given in Genesis 3:15, that the child would bruise the serpent's head, could point to the childbearing of Christ. According to Christian understanding, Christ is the only means of salvation from sin, and redemption is thus available through Christ for all of Eve's children. The problem with this interpretation, however, is that there are no other clues in the text that would lead us to limit this verse to Mary's childbearing of the Christ.

Another possibility is that salvation refers to preserving one's life through the birthing process. "Saved" could be translated as "brought safely through" or "delivered." In the ancient world, these definitions of "saved" were more widespread than the notion of being saved from sin. Women in the throes of childbirth frequently called upon mother goddesses, such as Artemis, for a safe delivery.[36] Such women would find it only natural to believe this verse meant they would be brought safely through the delivery of their children. Tying this idea back to verses 13-14, we know the consequences of Eve's sin in Genesis 3:16 was difficult childbirth. Jewish tradition further developed the so-called "curse" to include the possibility of death during childbirth. Here, Paul could have been promising that Christian women, who lived under the new covenant, would experience safe delivery of their children rather than the consequences of the fall. It was a lifting of part of the "curse" for women. This interpretation, however, does not stand up to reality. Devoted Christian women have died in childbirth, and most non-Christian women have survived childbirth.

A third possible interpretation involves the Greek word *soteria.* Often translated as "salvation," the word can also mean "preservation" or "release." Taking the translation "preservation," the verse could mean that women would be "preserved" by fulfilling the roles expected of them in their culture. This interpretation fits in well with the second half of the verse, which includes the word *sophrosyne,* interpreted here as "self-restraint," but the word also carried ideas of propriety. In the Greco-Roman and Jewish world of the first century, propriety for women included domestic roles and bearing children.[37]

This interpretation probably fits in best with what was happening in the Ephesian congregation. Some people were forbidding marriage (1 Tim 4:3). One could infer from 1 Timothy 5:14-15 that some women were not getting married, having children, or keeping house due to the influences of a false teaching.

The false teachings concerning marriage and childbearing also may have been Gnostic. Gnostics reportedly believed that all physical matter was evil. Because physical material was considered evil, trapping a soul in a physical body through childbirth also was seen as evil.[38] There probably were some early teachings circulating among the Ephesian women that Jesus had done away with the works of women, including childbearing (as in the Gospel according to the Egyptians),[39] and that to be saved, women had to become like males (as in the Gospel of Thomas and the Gospel of Mary).[40]

Along with possible Gnostic influences may have come influences from members of the Artemis cult, who promoted sexual abstinence.[41] In addition, there is another clue to the interpretation of this verse found in the address to the Ephesian church in Revelation 2:6: "Yet this is to your credit: you hate the works of the Nicolaitans, which I also hate." Nicolaitans held Gnostic beliefs that were later inherited by the Phibionites. The Phibionites strongly opposed procreation.[42] It is quite possible, then, that the Nicolaitans in Ephesus were opposed to childbearing and were spreading their false teachings among members of the Christian congregation.

Given the overall context of this verse, it is conceivable that Paul was reaffirming sexual relations and the childbearing function for women in the Ephesian congregation.[43] He could be taking the opposite tack from the Gnostics by telling women that even if they bore children, they could still receive eternal life. Women did not have to reject their femininity and become like men; they did not have to give up marrying and bearing children so they could receive eternal life. Paul may have been saying, in effect, that women could remain women and be saved even if they bore children. The verse can be translated as "throughout" or "with" the childbearing because of the grammatical structure of the sentence.[44] He was promoting family values by restoring the dignity and worth of women's role as mothers.

This interpretation also fits with the idea of propriety. In the Greco-Roman world, a woman's worth was tied to her ability to have children. Most people living at that time believed the purpose of marriage was to bear and raise children. This idea was enforced by Roman legislation. Caesar Augustus gave penalties to women who were unmarried and childless by the age of twenty, as he wanted to keep as many women as possible pregnant and raising children. Paul probably didn't want the Romans to bring down persecution on the Ephesian congregation, so he encouraged the women to marry and have children. This way the congregation could look proper rather than scandalous in the eyes of Roman authorities.

Paul probably was trying to make it clear to these women that they would not lose their salvation by marrying and having children; and by doing so, they also would help the church prevent persecution from Roman authorities.

Although many of the women in the Ephesian church were being led astray by false doctrines, Paul attempted to provide them with a proper Christian education; forbade them to teach false ideas, such as the belief that Eve was created before Adam; warned the women of the consequences of being deceived, using Eve as an example; and affirmed that they could still receive salvation even if they had children. In short, Paul wanted these women to recognize their worth and dignity as women and, when properly educated, to return to their roles as a royal priesthood within the Ephesian congregation.

Questions for Reflection

1. If Paul was seeking to equalize the relationship between women and men by encouraging women to learn about their faith, what was he asking men to do in the following passages: 1 Timothy 3:4-5, 12; 5:14; Titus 1:6; 2:4? How would this have been a radical step for the Ephesian congregation?
2. Which interpretation of 1 Timothy 2:15 leaves you the most satisfied? Why?
3. Compare 1 Timothy 5:14, where Paul advises young widows to remarry and rear children, with his advice about marriage in 1 Corinthians 7.
4. How do you feel about women teaching men? Has that feeling changed since reading this chapter?
5. How do you feel about women having some authority over men in the church? Has that feeling changed since reading this chapter?

Notes

[1]Edgar Hennecke, *New Testament Apocrypha*, ed. Wilhelm Schneemelcher (Philadelphia: Westminster Press, 1965) 2:353-64.

[2]David Hugh Farmer, *The Oxford Dictionary of Saints* (Oxford: Clarendon Press, 1978) 369.

[3]Leonard Swidler, *Biblical Affirmations of Woman* (Philadelphia: Westminster Press, 1979) 318.

[4]Sharon Hodgin Gritz, *Paul, Women Teachers, and the Mother Goddess at Ephesus* (Lanham MD: University Press of America, 1991) 12.

[5]Catherine Clark Kroeger, "1 Tim 2:12—A Classicist's View," in Berkeley and Alvera Mickelsen, *Women, Authority, & the Bible* (Downers Grove IL: InterVarsity Press, 1986) 227.

[6]David George Hogarth, *Excavations at Ephesus: The Archaic Artemisia* (London: William Clowes and Sons, Ltd., 1908) 2.

[7]Koshi Usami, *Somatic Comprehension of Unity: The Church in Ephesus* (Rome: Biblical Institute Press, 1983) 15.

[8]Gritz, 41.

[9]Ibid., 13.

[10]Ibid., 43.

[11]Ibid., 35.

[12]Paul Jewett, *Man as Male and Female* (Grand Rapids: Wm. B. Eerdmans Publishing Co., 1975) 91.

[13]Aida Besancon Spencer, *Beyond the Curse: Women Called to Ministry* (Nashville: Thomas Nelson Publishers, 1985) 74-75.

[14]Spencer, 77; and Gritz, 129.

[15]Gritz, 128.

[16]Richard Clark Kroeger and Catherine Clark Kroeger, *I Suffer Not a Woman* (Grand Rapids: Baker Book House, 1992) 75-76; and Kroeger, 237.

[17]Kroeger and Kroeger, *I Suffer Not a Woman,* 75-76.

[18]Spencer, 85.

[19]Kroeger and Kroeger, *I Suffer Not a Woman,* 37.

[20]Ibid., 79; Kroeger and Kroeger, *"1 Tim 2:12–a Classicist's View,"* 225.

[21]Kroeger and Kroeger, *I Suffer Not a Woman,* 83.

[22]Ibid., 84.

[23]Spencer, 87.

[24]Kroeger and Kroeger, *I Suffer Not a Woman,* 99.

[25]Kroeger, "1 Tim 2:12—A Classicist's View," 229.

[26]Kroeger and Kroeger, *I Suffer Not a Woman,* 99.

[27]Ibid., 103, 191.

[28]Ibid., 149-50.

[29]Ibid., 118.

[30]Kroeger, "1 Tim 2:12—A Classicist's View," 233.

[31]Kroeger and Kroeger, *I Suffer Not a Woman,* 167.

[32]Ibid., 122.

[33]Ibid., 129.

[34]Gritz, 140.

[35]Kroeger and Kroeger, *I Suffer Not a Woman,* 122.

[36]Craig S. Keener, *Paul, Women, and Wives* (Peabody MA: Hendrickson Publishers, Inc., 1992) 118.

[37]Ibid.

[38]Kroeger and Kroeger, *I Suffer Not a Woman,* 174; Kroeger, "1 Tim 2:12—A Classicist's View," 243.

[39]Kroeger and Kroeger, *I Suffer Not a Woman,* 173; Kroeger, "1 Tim 2:12—A Classicist's View," 243.

[40]Ibid.

[41]Gritz, 115.

[42]Kroeger and Kroeger, *I Suffer Not a Woman,* 175.

[43]Kroeger, "1 Tim 2:12—A Classicist's View," 243; Gritz, 144; and Richard and Catherine Kroeger, *Women Elders . . . Sinners or Servants?* (New York: Council on Women and the Church of the United Presbyterian Church in the USA, 1981) 16.

[44]Kroeger and Kroeger, *I Suffer Not a Woman,* 176.

Chapter 9

A Household of Faith

1 Peter 3:1-9; Ephesians 5:21-33; Colossians 3:18-19

"He was very insecure. He wanted to control things to feel more secure. Once, when he beat me up, I thought I was dead. He talked about cutting off my head. He pulled out gobs of hair, chipped a tooth, cracked a rib, and beat me up really bad. I was so black and blue, you couldn't recognize me." These are the words of a Christian victim of domestic violence. Although this attack was one of many by a later boyfriend, she had been married to a physically abusive husband. She stayed in her marriage for years because she believed it was God's will.[1]

Lonnie Collins Pratt was married to a pastor and evangelist who beat her regularly. "I really believed that to end the marriage was to end any relationship with God," she recalls. "At one point I had a miscarriage because I had been beaten so badly." She finally went to another pastor for help, but he told her, "Go home and don't make him do this. How do you make him so angry?" She finally left her husband when she realized he wanted her to die.[2]

These victims of domestic violence are not alone, either in their beliefs or in being victims. Religious beliefs are just as important to abused Christian wives as to those not abused. Women who call shelters for help often express a belief in the Bible that dramatically complicates their dilemma. Most pastors deny there is domestic violence perpetrated against members of their congregations, even though almost one half of women experiencing physical abuse contact their pastors first for help.[3] And, there are plenty of Christian wives who are abused.

According to the U.S. Justice Department, 243,000 persons were treated in hospital emergency rooms for domestic violence injuries in 1994. Their injuries were inflicted by spouses, former spouses, or by current or former boyfriends or girlfriends. A higher percentage of the victims were women.[4] According to one survey, 1 of every 4 Methodist wives had been emotionally or verbally abused, and 1 of every 13 had been physically abused by their husbands.[5] According to FBI reports, 1/3 of women who are killed are murdered by either a spouse or an intimate acquaintance.[6] In fact, 3-4% of families experience the use of a weapon, punching, or kicking. Severe violence affects 1.8 million American families.[7] About ½ of battered women are beaten at least 3 times a year.[8]

Although men who batter blame the women for inciting them to behave abusively, women are not responsible for men's choices to batter, according to Rhonda Smith, victim's advocate for the Fayette County attorney's office in Lexington, Kentucky. "There is never an acceptable cause for violence," she said.

Perpetrators commonly have irritable depression and anxiety, according to Robert Walker, MSW, LCSW.[9] "They are unhappy men who seek to meld the world to their expectations to escape their own inadequacies," he said. "They tend to project their failures onto others, particularly spouses and children, and then expect others to meet their needs in ways they dictate."

Violent men batter because they have a strong need to control others, especially those who are personally important to them, according to Walker. "The perpetrator believes that his wife and children are supposed to be subordinate to his will and inclinations. The perpetrator cannot bear the thought of the loss of his partner, nor can he tolerate behavior from her that suggests he is not in control."

Some men use a traditional interpretation of the Bible's Household Codes to justify their violence against women. However, the Bible neither supports nor condones violence in the home, male use of Scripture to control the behavior of wives, or the inordinate submission of women to the wills of their husbands. In fact, the domination of men over women is sin. God created women and men to be equals. For a husband to lord it over his wife is a direct violation of God's plan at creation.

The Bible and Abuse

A careful reading of Scripture shows that God is opposed to violence because violence is sin (Gen 6:11). In fact, when the earth was filled with violence, God destroyed all the inhabitants except Noah and his family. God is always on the side of the oppressed and downtrodden. God championed the Israelites when they were enslaved to and abused by Pharaoh in Egypt. With God's help, the Israelites were able to escape from their powerful oppressors. God championed the cause of Hannah when Penninnah verbally abused her, and God vindicated her with a son. Hannah acknowledged the power of God to strengthen the feeble and bring down the proud (1 Sam 1–2:10). God also championed widows and orphans, and promised to rise in anger against those who sought to hurt them (Exod 22:22-24). Psalm 73 was the prayer of someone victimized by the violence of those who held power over him, and the writer acknowledged that God despised their evil ways.

The prayers of Hannah and of the psalmist reveal their strong belief in their own self-worth in the eyes of God. They knew they were loved and valued by God and that their oppressors' behavior was wrong. They knew God wanted them to be free of their painful situations. The prophet Isaiah repeated this theme in Isaiah 61, revealing once again that God wants liberty for those held captive and desires freedom for prisoners. Jesus carried this idea forward into the Gospels when he read Isaiah's passage in the Nazarene synagogue (Luke 4:16-21).

Jesus encouraged his disciples to be wise as serpents and harmless as doves and to beware of men (Matt 10:16-17), making it clear that there are plenty of people who simply cannot be trusted. Jesus was so angry about the injustices of the money-changers in the temple that he overturned their tables and threw them out (Matt 21:12-13), making him a source for righteous anger for those who are abused and treated unjustly.[10] Jesus even broke Old Testament law to prevent violence against a woman. The woman caught in adultery was spared execution (John 7:53–8:11) when Jesus affirmed her personhood and her value in the eyes of God. Then Jesus set her free.

Jesus further encouraged his followers to leave those who did not value them. His followers were those who heard and did the word (Mark 8:34-35), including women. Jesus told his disciples to shake the dust from their feet and leave the places where they were not valued (Luke 9:1-5). He gave the disciples the power and authority to obey Christ in such instances. So, too, women followers of Jesus received the power and authority to shake the dust off their feet and leave situations where they were not valued. This way, they could experience healing for themselves, whether physical, emotional, or mental.

Certainly healing is important for those who experience violence. Violence can be seen as demonic, especially for those living with abusers and caught in what is called the cycle of violence. The women quoted at the opening of this chapter described predicaments that were obviously evil. Jesus came to cast out evil and to heal the hurting. If evil behavior continues, there is no healing. Certainly victims of violence have Christ's loving support to leave their situations so the evil will not continue in their lives. By getting out, they will be casting evil out of their lives so Christ can more fully enter in and heal them.

Household Codes

So what does a Christian wife, especially one being abused, do about the Bible's Household Codes, which tell women to submit to their husbands?

The Household Codes appear in three places in the New Testament (1 Pet 3:1-9; Eph 5:21-33; Col 3:18-19), yet these codes had actually existed for hundreds of years before Christ, though in various forms. The three pairs mentioned as part of the Household Codes—how the male would rule his wife, his children, and his slaves—probably originated with Aristotle's writings. Aristotle, a fourth-century B.C.E. Greek philosopher, also taught that women were inferior to men and should be ruled by them. His beliefs gained widespread appeal in the ancient world.[11] The later teachings of both Josephus and Philo, who were Jews, included the belief that wives were to be subject to their husbands, and children were to obey their parents. According to Roman law, husbands were to rule over their wives and were totally responsible for their wives' behavior.[12] Wives were, therefore, required by law to submit to their husbands' wishes.[13] The ancient Household Codes generally did not suggest husbands were to love or submit to their wives.[14]

Christianity, however, had a different view of household relationships. Following the example of Jesus, Christians attempted to set up a new household of faith—a family of equals with no father-figure except God. All believers were to be treated as equals before God (Eph 2:11-22; 4:4-6; 1 Cor 12:13; Gal 3:28). This idea made Christianity very attractive to women and slaves, who could join and experience a new kind of freedom. The conservative male establishment, however, found such prospects threatening. There is evidence for this attitude found in the attacks against Christianity written in the second and third centuries C.E. These attacks included accusations that Christians were threatening societal order and were subverting the traditional household system.[15]

Christians had to do something to curb these attacks on their faith and to make Christianity more winsome to the surrounding culture. Given their small numbers and precarious position in Roman-controlled territory, challenging the views of society would have been both dangerous and futile.[16] Therefore, to reduce persecution against the church, the writers of the Epistles wisely borrowed ideas from their culture and modified them.

The writers of the Epistles probably encouraged Christians to live by the societal Household Codes for more than one reason. First, by following these codes, Christians would be able to prevent some persecution from the Romans. Members of the Roman upper class suspected the Christians were undermining traditional family values, especially when Roman women converted to Christianity.[17] In a Roman family, the wife was required to adopt the religion of her husband. If she converted to Christianity, she threatened the household order and was not upholding her family's traditions.[18] If Christian wives submitted to their husbands, as all Roman women were expected to do, then charges that Christianity destroyed the Roman "family values" of that period could be silenced. The writers of the Epistles, therefore, encouraged wives to maintain the Roman tradition of submission to their husbands to prevent persecution.

Second, if members of the church followed the traditional Roman cultural values—modified to coincide with the new faith—Christianity would appear less threatening and more appealing to the Romans.[19] Christian women often had pagan husbands who expected them to behave in a submissive manner. If these women continued with their submissive behavior, they had a better chance of gaining a hearing from the men. Challenging the Roman law of male authority in the household would have brought down condemnation and possibly divorce on a wife, ending any chance for converting the husband. Divorced women in antiquity were usually poor women. The typical "profession" for poor single women was prostitution because they usually had little other means for earning a living. Therefore, the writers of the Epistles encouraged wives to stay and continue with the customs of their households.

1 Peter 3

The Household Codes were copied by both Peter and Paul. Peter used them as a tool for evangelization in his first letter to some churches in a Greek province that was under Roman rule. These Christians were being persecuted (1 Pet 3:14) and needed to do whatever it took within the realm of Christian conscience to keep out of trouble (2:11-12; 3:16). Peter encouraged Christians to follow the Roman laws and societal norms to avoid unnecessary persecution. Therefore, Peter encouraged wives to submit to their non-Christian husbands in an effort to win those men to Christ (3:1).

While Roman law already required wives to submit to their husbands, Peter added a new twist to it. Although the Christians were not in a position to change the Roman laws, they did have a choice about how they would follow the law. Peter was probably well aware of how some women submitted to their husbands, and it probably was not chaste or respectful. Some may have submitted with an attitude of resentful bitterness; some may have submitted in an attempt to appease or placate angry husbands; some probably submitted out of a sense of low self-worth; and some may have readily submitted while subversively planning to manipulate or control their situations. Peter reached beyond the petty, worldly, or devaluing forms of submission and asked women to submit to their husbands with chaste and respectful behavior. Such behavior would be fitting for a Christian in Roman society, especially a Christian woman living with an unbelieving husband.

When speaking of submission, Peter referred to women's adornment: hairstyles, clothing, and jewelry. His reference probably pointed to the behavior of the elite Roman women, whose main pastime was getting stylishly dressed, going to the public baths, and getting fancily dressed again for the trip home.[20] Peter wanted the Christian women to avoid such conspicuous displays of wealth. Instead, he wanted them to focus on developing the Christian virtues of a gentle and quiet spirit, to be submissive, as Roman law required, and to become more winsome to their non-Christian husbands.

For his example of submission, Peter referred in 1 Peter 3:6 to Sarah obeying Abraham. However, there are no obvious instances in the Old Testament of Sarah obeying a command from Abraham. Rather, the reverse is true: Abraham obeyed Sarah. In Genesis 21:12, God told Abraham to do whatever Sarah told him to do. Sarah decided to evict Hagar and Ishmael, a choice that sealed the fate of both the Israelites and the Arabs. Despite Abraham's distress at losing his firstborn son, he submitted to Sarah's wish, following the will of God. Sarah did call Abraham "lord," or *adonia* (Gen 18:12). The term *adonia* did not imply that Abraham lorded it over Sarah, but was a term used to indicate respect, like "sir," or used as a synonym for "husband."[21] Peter was pointing out that Sarah treated her husband with respect.

Peter never told women to obey their husbands. Peter did, in fact, tell the early church members to "obey God rather than men." (Acts 5:29 NASB) Likewise, Peter never told husbands how to rule or govern their wives, nor did he give the men authority over their wives. He never set up any hierarchical arrangements in the household. Instead, he told husbands to live with their wives in an understanding way and to grant them honor. To honor someone means to show them great respect or high regard. By honoring their wives, these men would have free access to God in prayer. In addition, Peter called husbands and wives joint heirs of the grace of life; they can't very well be joint heirs if they are not equals before God.

Beyond marital relationships, Peter asked all Christians to refrain from speaking evil or guile, to turn away from evil and do good, and to pursue peace and to do what is right. In addition, he implored Christians to be harmonious, sympathetic, brotherly, kindhearted, and humble in spirit. Husbands and wives, as Christians, would be expected to treat each other as well as all other people with the same loving respect. If couples treated each other this way, there would be no abuse in marriages.

Ephesians 5

The theme of mutual love and respect between spouses is repeated in Paul's version of the Household Codes in Ephesians 5. Following a theme of unity, he encouraged the Ephesians to love each other as Christ loved them (v. 2). Then, he introduced a section describing the behavior of those who are filled with the Spirit: They speak in psalms and hymns and spiritual songs, they sing and make melody with their hearts, they give thanks, and they are subject to one another. Paul's point was to describe the behavior that flows out of the mutual love and caring that is to be shared among Christians who are filled with the Spirit (v. 18). This behavior was not just for church, but extended into the home.

Paul encouraged mutual submission out of reverence for Christ (v. 21). This echoed his letter to the Galatians, when he asked the Christians there to be slaves (*douloi*) for each other and to fulfill the whole law by loving their neighbors as they loved themselves (5:13-14). Paul did not write this as a governing ideal just for relationships in the church; it included marital relationships. He told all Christians, including spouses, to practice two-way submission, which implied equality and no hierarchical organization, even within the marital relationship.

Next, Paul wrote, "Wives, be subject to your husbands as you are to the Lord" (v. 22). The words "be subject," commonly included in English translations, are not found in the original Greek. So, what are wives to do to their husbands? To get the answer, we must refer back to verse 21. Here, Paul told all Christians to be subject to each other. The Greek word translated "submit" is *hupotassomenoi,* and it was written in the middle voice. This meant submitting was what one did to one's self. Paul was asking Christians to submit freely and voluntarily to each other, with no one receiving any preferential treatment. No coercion and no authority figures were involved; there was no hierarchy or chain of command mentioned. So, verse 22 becomes a further explanation of verse 21. Wives are only some of those who are to be subject; and if all are to be subject to each other, then husbands must also be subject to their wives.

Paul told wives how they were to be subject to their husbands: not just as those following Roman law, but as to the Lord. This doesn't mean a woman's husband is a lord she must submit to; God is her only Lord. This verse refers to the quality of her self-submission to her husband as she submits to the Lord; by responding to love with loving and devoted service. Therefore, Paul was asking wives to be subject to their husbands by responding to their love with loving service. He was not asking for the subjection of a slave who lives under the authority of an oppressive master, or even for the wife to obey, but for the subjection that is the natural response of a mutually submissive couple who love each other.

Husbands and Heads

Paul went on to explain why wives were to be subject to their husbands. "For the husband is the head of the wife just as Christ is the head of the church, the body of which he is the Savior" (v. 23). The husband was head of the wife, but that did not necessarily mean he was her authority. As in 1 Corinthians 11, the word *kephale,* translated "head," did not indicate "authority" during that time in history. Rather, it indicated a source, such as headwaters or a fountainhead. The husband was the source of the wife in the sense that *ha-adam* was the source for the woman in Genesis 2:21-24. Paul made this reference clear in Ephesians 5:31 when he repeated Genesis 2:24, and also in Ephesians 1:22 and 4:15-16.

In Ephesians 1:22, Paul uses two metaphors to explain the relationship of Christ to the church. In the first metaphor, he says all things are under subjection to Christ by being under Christ's feet. In other words, Christ has authority over all things. Here, Paul is explaining a relationship of the authority of Christ and the subjection of the church.

In the second metaphor, Christ is described as having another relationship to the church: He is the head of the body, and the body is the church. We know this is a second metaphor, explaining a second relationship, because the church cannot be both Christ's body and under his feet at the same time. The verse is not saying Christ is an authority over his body, because Christ is already the authority over all things that are under his feet. Rather, this is a metaphor for yet another way Christ relates to the church. Paul explained this other relationship in verse 23: Christ fills his body—the church—with his fullness. Here the function of Christ as head is to provide the church with fullness; Christ is, therefore, the source of life and nurturance for the church. This makes Christ the source for the church, just as headwaters are the source of a river. As head, Christ's role is to supply the church with its needs, not to rule it as an authority.

The concept of Christ as head appears again in Ephesians 4:15-16. Here, Christ as head is described as one who causes the church to grow. Christ as head is not the authority over its growth. Once again, no reference to Christ as authority over the church is made when Christ is referred to as the head of the church.

In Ephesians 5:23, therefore, a precedent is already set for the definition of head: as Christ is head or source for the church, so also the husband is head or source for the wife. Here, Christ is the source of salvation for the church and is a servant to the church. Christ gave himself up for the church (v. 25) and nourishes and cherishes the church (v. 29). There is no indication in the text that Christ as head of the church is the ruler or authority over the church. Rather, as head, Christ is the source of nourishment and salvation for the church.

If Christ is the head of the church in the sense of being its authority or ruler, then Paul logically would have gone on to explain that husbands, as heads of their wives, are to rule or have authority over their wives and to keep their wives subject. Yet, Paul said nothing of the kind. Instead, Paul told husbands to love their wives and to be servants to their wives. To be another's servant is to submit to that person. Therefore, Paul discreetly encouraged husbands to submit to their wives.

Because Paul focused on two-way submission, he went far beyond what the other ancient writers had required of husbands. While law and society told husbands to rule their wives and said nothing about love, Paul had a more Christlike interpretation of how marital relationships would work.

If husbands behave in self-sacrificing and loving ways to their wives, as Paul encouraged them to do, then the natural response of loving wives would be to submit to them in return. This is the mutual submission Paul spoke of: be subject to one another (v. 21).

God calls men to be subject to their wives, thereby loving their wives as Christ loves the church. Christ loved the church enough to die for it. Christ had the power to avoid death on the cross, yet he chose not to exercise that power but to submit to the events taking place and to human authority figures. Likewise, Paul was addressing men who lived in a culture that gave them absolute power in a marriage. Paul urged men to let go of that power and live as though it didn't exist by giving up their legal rights and sacrificing or submitting to the point of death for their wives. This would create a balance of power in the marriage relationship, as well as greater possibilities for love between the spouses. In contrast, a man who sets himself up as his wife's ruler or dictator warps the intent of this passage. It also would mock the example of Christ who humbled himself, becoming a servant even to the point of being crucified.

Christ, however, continued beyond the ultimate sacrifice of his death to infuse the church with holiness, bringing the church into the fullness of glory. The husband's responsibility also extends beyond sacrifice. If he follows the example of Christ (Eph 5:1, 2), then he will work to help bring about a positive transformation in his wife. His work is to help his wife become sanctified, enabling her to become holy and blameless, coming into Christian glory. A woman who is holy and living the fullness of God's glory is a woman who has been made whole and complete in Christ; she will be a woman who loves God with all her heart, soul, mind, and strength, and a woman who loves her fellow human beings with the fullness with which she is called to love herself (Matt 22:37-40; Mark 12:29-31).

Husbands and Bodies

Paul further elaborated that husbands are to love their wives as their own bodies, an idea that reflects the mutual authority wives and husbands are called to have over each others' bodies (1 Cor 7:4). In addition, Paul's repetition of Genesis 2:24 indicated Paul was encouraging men and women to live together in unity and equality as God designed men and women to live.

Paul explained that all Christians are members of Christ's body, and his body is to be nourished and cherished (vv. 29-30). Husbands and wives are called upon to nourish and cherish each other just as Christ nourishes and cherishes them. A husband who dominates or humiliates his wife is not keeping the principle of mutual submission. Rather, husbands are to love their wives, and wives are to respect their husbands. Likewise, wives who respect their husbands will refrain from humiliating or depreciating them.

Here is a picture of Christ as the source of life, growth, nurturance, and self-sacrifice for the church, and the church responding with loving submission by growing into the fullness of Christ. As though a mirror-image of this model, husbands are to be a source of love and nurturance for their wives, submitting themselves by sacrificing to help their wives reach their own fullness as whole persons in Christ. A wife who is loved this much probably will respond joyfully with love and respect and a desire to serve her husband. This loving response will not arise out of selfish desires, the need to appease, the powerlessness of resignation, or feelings of low self-worth. Instead, it will flow with celebration out of a heart that is full of love and emotional health.[22]

To emphasize his point, Paul called the concept of mutual submission a "mystery" (v. 32). In his day, a mystery was a truth that had just been revealed. The idea of wifely submission was not new; the idea of mutual submission and the call for husbands to love their wives was new.[23] The truth of mutual submission within the marriage relationship was now to become a reality. This mutual submission was to be a signpost to the world that God was at the center of their marriage; that these Christians were following the divine pattern of mutuality and equality, and reflecting the divine order of mutual sacrifice and love (Eph 5:1, 2). This divine order was established in creation and followed through with Christ's redemption, making mutual submission a fundamental principle in the way Christians relate to each other.

While the focus of traditional interpretations of this passage tends to put the spotlight on women, the Greek actually focuses on the behavior of the husbands. Paul used ninety-two words to give instructions to the men, but only used forty words in his guidance for the women. Clearly, his focus was on male behavior in the Ephesian community.

Paul summarized this passage by telling men to love their wives as themselves and telling wives to respect their husbands (v. 33). If husband and wife are practicing mutual submission, it is to be done out of love and respect. In Paul's summary, he does not tell husbands how to behave as the authority over their wives, but as one loving himself, for she is flesh of his flesh and bone of his bone. Likewise, Paul does not tell wives to obey their husbands, but to treat them with respect so they are not humiliated. Paul indicates that this behavior is to be carried out with all humility and gentleness, with patience and forbearance. The end result is unity and peace, a oneness of body and of spirit (Eph 4:1-4).

Colossians 3:18-19; Titus 2:5

Paul gives a greatly shortened version of the Household Codes in his letters to the church in Colossae and to Titus. In these passages, he encourages wives to be subject to their husbands, as is fitting in the Lord and so the word of God may not be dishonored. This means wives are to respond to the love of God by providing loving and devoted service to their husbands. Again, Paul is not requiring wives to live as slaves under an oppressive master, but to do their part by being submissive out of love. Likewise, Paul tells the husbands to love their wives, not to rule over them or treat them poorly. To love is to submit to the needs of the other, creating a mutually submissive relationship based on love rather than power.

The Slavery Example

One other idea about the Household Codes should be kept in mind. About 150 years ago, the Bible was used by well-meaning Christians, such as Bishop John England in the United States Catholic Miscellany and the Baptist Richard Furman, to perpetuate slavery.[24] Christians used the following Scriptures to support their proslavery stance: Leviticus 25:44-46, Matthew 8:9-13, Luke 17:7-10, 1 Corinthians 7:20-24, Ephesians 6:5-8, 1 Timothy 6:1-2. Note the Household Codes (Eph 6:5-8; 1 Pet 2:18-19) were used to require the obedience of slaves. The theology of slavery was hardly questioned, even though Christians had a history of God releasing the Israelites from slavery in Egypt. In fact, when some Christians rose up about 150 years ago to denounce slavery, they were accused of denying the authority of the Bible.[25] Yet today, most Christians realize that slavery is a clear violation of Christian principles.

Similarly, traditional biblical interpretation has supported the idea that women are to be subject to the authority of their husbands. Those who have called such interpretations into question in recent decades have been accused of not accepting the authority of God's Word, just as those who opposed slavery were criticized.

If Christians are to follow the traditional interpretations about the role of wives in marriage, then they also must be willing to accept the reinstatement of slavery. Yet, with modern interpretation, they need not. The passages directed toward the slaves were designed to comfort them in a situation that could not be changed. Paul himself freed a slave woman from her spirit of divination (Acts 16:18-21), thereby violating her owners' legal rights to make a profit from her ability.[26] Clearly, the intent of God is to rid the world of slavery. If Paul could ask slaves to obey their masters, yet not be a supporter of slavery, so, too, he could ask wives to submit without supporting the idea of husbands being authorities over their wives,[27] as was legally the case in his day. Christians today acknowledge that slavery is wrong, even though the Household Codes appear to support it. It took almost two millennia after Christ for society to rid itself of slavery.

Likewise, the Household Codes directed toward wives were written to help women cope with their reality of required submission by Roman law. What lay next to this requirement was the new, radical idea that Christian husbands also were to love and submit to their wives rather than control them. Perhaps this concept of mutual submission was so radical for the Christians that the church eventually lost sight of this teaching and reverted to the behavior of the surrounding culture—insisting only on the submission of wives, but not that of husbands. The chaos and pain that started in the Garden of Eden had continued, while the mutuality and equality of the first couple were forgotten.

This might not be the end of the story, however. In recent centuries, Christian principles of love have defeated the belief that slavery is God's will. Soon, perhaps, Christian principles of mutual submission and love might also win out for women in oppressive relationships.[28]

Questions for Reflection

1. How have 1 Peter 3, Ephesians 5, and Colossians 3 been interpreted to you in the past? How did it make you feel about God?
2. How do those interpretations compare to what you read in this chapter? Which seem to be more in line with Christ's teachings?
3. Does Philippians 2:3-8 affect spousal relationships? If so, how?
4. Can you accept the definition of head as source? Why or why not?
5. If you are married, how do you and your spouse resolve differences? Can this be improved upon? If so, how? How can spiritual gifts be used to resolve differences between spouses? (See Rom 12:3-6; 1 Cor 12:4-7.)
6. If you are married, but you and your spouse do not currently practice mutual submission but began to, would your marriage be different? If so, how?
7. In what ways can decision-making responsibilities be divided between spouses?
8. Do you believe a woman who is the victim of domestic violence has God's approval to leave her situation? Why or why not?

9. Do you perceive domestic violence as a problem in your home? In your church? In your community? If so, what can be done about it?
10. If you are married, in what ways do you submit to your spouse? In what ways does your spouse submit to you? Are these ways mutually satisfactory? If not, what can you do collectively or individually to improve the situation for either or both of you?
11. If you are married and the two of you reach an impasse, how can Luke 14:31-32 and Acts 6:1-6 and 15:37-40 help you and your spouse find middle ground and negotiate a compromise?

Notes

[1]Heidi Bright Parales, "Domestic Violence: Two UK Women Tell Their Stories," *communi-K.* 28, no. 8 (18 January 1996): 7.

[2]Linda Midgett, "Silent Screams: Are Evangelicals Responding Effectively to Abused Women?" *Christianity Today,* 19 July 1993, 44.

[3]Carole R. Bohn, "Dominion to Rule," Joanne Carlson Brown and Carole R. Bohn, eds., *Christianity, Patriarchy, and Abuse: A Feminist Critique* (New York: The Pilgrim Press, 1989) 112.

[4]Jube Shiver, Jr., "243,000 Treated for Domestic Violence," *The Lexington Herald-Leader,* 25 August 1997, A-1.

[5]Susan Brooks Thistlethwaite, "Every Two Minutes: Battered Women and Feminist Interpretation," Letty M. Russell, ed., *Feminist Interpretation of the Bible* (Philadelphia: Westminster Press, 1985) 96.

[6]Alexis Jetter, "How Battered Wives Can Learn to Leave," *McCall's,* September 1994, 104.

[7]Murray A. Straus and Richard A. Gelles, National Family Violence Survey, sponsored by the National Institute of Mental Health.

[8]Bryan Strong and Christine DeVault, *The Marriage and Family Experience* (St. Paul MN: West Publishing Company, 1995) 490.

[9]Robert Walker, MSW, LCSW, is director of the Comprehensive Care Center, Lexington, KY, a clinic offering treatment services to victims and perpetrators of domestic violence. Walker also is assistant professor in the College of Social Work with a clinical faculty appointment in the department of psychiatry in the College of Medicine at the University of Kentucky in Lexington.

[10]Marie F. Fortune, "The Transformation of Suffering," *Christianity, Patriarchy, and Abuse: A Feminist Critique,* 141.

[11]Craig S. Keener, *Paul, Women, and Wives* (Peabody MA: Hendrickson Publishers, Inc. 1992) 146.

[12]Ibid., 146, 165.

[13]Patricia Gundry, *Woman, Be Free!* (Grand Rapids: Zondervan Publishing House, 1977) 72.

[14]Keener, 167.

[15]Elisabeth Schüssler Fiorenza, *In Memory of Her* (New York: The Crossroad Publishing Co, Inc., 1983) 265.

[16]Keener, 159.

[17]Ibid., 133.

[18]Fiorenza, 263-64; and Keener, 142.

[19]Keener, 147.

[20]Gundry, 82.

[21]Brown, Driver, Briggs, and Gesenius, *A Hebrew and English Lexicon of the Old Testament* (Oxford: Clarendon Press, 1979) 11. See also E. Margaret Howe, *Women and Church Leadership* (Grand Rapids: Zondervan Publishing House, 1982) 56.

[22]Gilbert Bilizekian, *Beyond Sex Roles: A Guide for the Study of Female Roles in the Bible* (Grand Rapids: Baker Book House, 1985) 167.

[23]Ibid., 164.

[24]Gundry, 52.

[25]Alvin J. Schmidt, *Veiled and Silenced: How Culture Shaped Sexist Theology* (Macon GA: Mercer University Press, 1989) 30.

[26]Fiorenza, 265.

[27]Keener, 135.

[28]Paul Jewett, *Man as Male and Female* (Grand Rapids: Wm. B. Eerdmans Publishing Co., 1975) 12.

Chapter 10

The Image of God

"And so in our making, God almighty is our loving Father, and God all wisdom is our loving Mother, with the love and the goodness of the Holy Spirit, which is all one God, one Lord. . . . So Jesus Christ, who opposes good to evil, is our true Mother. We have our being from him, where the foundation of motherhood begins, with all the sweet protection of love which endlessly follows. As truly as God is our Father, so truly is God our Mother. . . . My kind Mother, my gracious Mother, my beloved Mother, have mercy on me."

—Julian of Norwich[1]

Others who have referred to God as mother include: Clement of Alexandria (Greek theologian, 150–215), Origen (theologian and scholar, 185–254), Irenaeus (father of Catholic theology, d. ca. 200), St. John Chrysostom (Patriarch of Constantinople, 347–407), Synesius of Cyrene (bishop of Ptolemais at Lybia, ca. 370–ca. 414), St. Gregory of Nyssa (bishop of Cappadocia, d. ca. 395), St. Augustine of Hippo (354–430), The Venerable Bede (English historian Benedictine monk, ca. 673–735), Benedictine St. Anselm (Archbishop of Canterbury, 1033–1109), Bernard of Clairvaux (founder of a Cistercian monastery, canonized by the Catholic Church, ca. 1090–1153), Guerric of Igny (a Cistercian father, d. ca. 1157), Peter Lombard (Archbishop of Paris, 1110–1164), William of St. Thierry (abbot of St. Thierry, 1075/80–1148), Aelred of Rievaulx (abbot of Rievaulx, 1109–1167), Isaac of Stella (Cistercian monk and abbot of Stella, ca. 1100–ca. 1178), Adam of Perseigne (d. 1221), Helinand of Froidmont (Cistercian monk, ca. 1160–ca. 1230), St. Bonaventure (cardinal bishop of Albano and Doctor of the Church, 1221–1274), Thomas Aquinas (Italian Dominican monk, theologian and philosopher, Doctor of the Church, 1225–1274), Angela of Foligno (Umbrian mystic, 1248–1309), St. Gregory Palamas (theologian and Archbishop of Thessaloniki, 1296–1359), St. Bridget of Sweden (patron saint of Sweden, ca. 1302–1373), St. Catherine of Siena (canonized and made a Doctor of the Church, 1347–1380), Margery Kempe (mystic of Norfolk England, ca. 1373–after 1438), St. Theresa of Avila (Spanish Carmelite nun, 1515–1582), Count Nikolaus Zinzendorf, Lutheran pietist leader and founder of the Moravian Church (1741).[2]

These Christians used the word mother as a metaphor for God. A metaphor is a figure of speech containing an implied comparison, in which a word or phrase ordinarily used of one thing is applied to another. For example, "the pearly gates of heaven" is a metaphor that uses something literal and physical we can understand (a gate encrusted with pearls) to describe something we don't understand (how we enter heaven). We can experience a literal gate encrusted with pearls. We have no reference point for entering heaven; it is outside our realm of experience. So, we use a metaphor to communicate the idea to others, and they understand more fully.

Christians use metaphors to talk about God, because God is ultimately incomprehensible to us. Through the use of metaphors, or picture-language, we can describe what we understand about God to help us search more deeply into the spiritual meaning behind the metaphor. Through the use of a metaphor, we can better understand who God is—yet also what God is not. God is our father, yet also is not our father. God is our father in the sense that God created humanity and is the source of our being; yet God is not our father because God did not have intercourse with our biological mother to create us.

The danger of metaphors for God comes in taking them literally, instead of seeing them as a compass pointing us in the right direction. When a metaphor is taken literally, it is no longer a metaphor, and the idea becomes literalized. One example would be seeing God literally as our father, a male being. Concretizing God as a father takes the mystery out of our experience of God, and then God becomes very limited in our minds. The God we then worship is not the one true God, but rather an idolatrous image of God based on our limited understanding.[3]

Persons in Christian history who referred to God as mother expanded their understanding of God beyond the obvious biblical references. They experienced a feminine side to God, based on their understanding of the Scriptures and their prayer life with God. They knew God was not their mother in the literal sense—that God was not the human woman who had intercourse and physically carried and gave birth to them. Rather, they used the word mother in a broader, more figurative sense; they used it as a metaphor. They looked at the positive attributes of human mothers and said that God, who is ultimately indescribable, has those positive attributes as well. Therefore, they felt comfortable using the metaphor of mother for God.

God as Father

For many today, it is unthinkable to entertain the idea that God might relate to us as both a mother and a father. The image of God as father has been with us for thousands of years, and this is what most Christians feel comfortable with. Yet the father image of God also is a metaphor. God is not a physical human male who impregnates a human female so she can give birth to us. Someone who uses the image of God as father takes the human attributes of a father and says God has those attributes as well, in an attempt to better understand God.

The Old Testament does describe God as a father, but only fourteen times. In none of the references is anyone directly addressing God as father. Of those fourteen references, five are about God's unique relationship with a king (God and King David—2 Sam 7:14; 1 Chron 17:13; Ps 89:26-29; God and King Solomon—1 Chron 22:10; 28:6), not with an ordinary person. In Malachi 1:6, God is addressing God's relationship with the priests: "A son honors his father, and servants their master. If then I am a father, where is the honor due me? And if I am a master, where is the respect due me? says the Lord of hosts to you, O priests, who despise my name."

The term father is used twice as a comparison, not as a direct address. In Deuteronomy 1:31, God is compared to a man who carries his son. In Psalm 103:13, God is compared to a father having compassion on his children: "As a father has compassion on his children, so the Lord has compassion for those who fear him." In both cases, God is not called a father, but is shown to share the compassion of a human father.

Now we come to the passages that make a more direct association to God as father. These passages present the idea that God created and brought forth life. As we read these passages about God as father, we must keep in mind that at the time, all people believed the physical father was the only one who created a new baby; the male planted his seed in the woman's garden, where the seed grew into a baby.[4] They were not aware that the woman contributed an ovum to create the child; the ovum was not even discovered until the nineteenth century.[5] Therefore, it was natural for the Israelites to understand that their ultimate source was a father image, not a mother image.

The father image is used twice in the Song of Moses: "Is not he your father, who created you, who made you and established you?" (Deut 32:6b). "You were unmindful of the Rock that bore you; you forgot the God who gave you birth. The Lord saw it, and was jealous he spurned his sons and daughters" (Deut 32:18-19). The father image also is evident in Jeremiah: "For I have become a father to Israel, and Ephraim is my firstborn" (31:9). The fatherhood of God, as creator of humans, extends beyond Israel in Malachi 2:10. "Have we not all one father? Has not one God created us?"

The other two references in the Old Testament to God as father are in the context of Israel spurning God's love. In Isaiah 63:16, the Israelites are calling out to God: "You are our father, though Abraham does not know us and Israel does not acknowledge us; you, O Lord, are our father; our Redeemer from of old is your name." In Jeremiah 3:4 and 19, Israel is faithless, and God is calling the nation back, as the father in the New Testament yearns for the return of the prodigal son who strayed:

> Have you not just now called to me, "My Father, you are the friend of my youth?" . . . I thought how I would set you among my children, and give you a pleasant land, the most beautiful heritage of all the nations. And I thought you would call me, My Father, and would not turn from following me.

The father in the prodigal son story in the New Testament gives an excellent picture of the nature of God as our metaphorical father—the father Jesus taught his disciples to address when praying (Matt 6:9; Luke 11:2). This father is not domineering, controlling, demanding, or punishing. Rather, this father respects individual freedom, waits with infinite patience, and receives love as a gift. This father treats his children as adults.

Jesus extended this view of the fatherhood of God by referring to God as *Abba* (Mark 14:36). This word embraces feelings of respect, love, and emotional intimacy, and was used by adult men when addressing their loving fathers. This is how Jesus viewed his Father, even while in the Garden of Gethsemane just before being taken prisoner.

God as Transcendent

God is careful, though, not to let this metaphor of fatherhood go too far; God does not want humans to literalize the metaphor. In the Old Testament, God says, "For I am God and no man (*ish,* the Hebrew word for a male), the Holy One in your midst" (Hos 11:9 NASB). The Hebrew word *ish* is specifically used in this verse to let the Israelites know that God is not a male. Earlier, the prophet Balaam said, "God is not a man (*ish*), that he should lie, nor a son of man (*adam*, or humanity), that he should repent" (Num 23:19 NASB).

God describes God's self not as human, but as Spirit (John 4:24) and as a verb of being: I AM WHO I AM (Exod 3:14). God also makes it clear that we are not to identify God with anything else, including human males: "To whom then will you compare me, or who is my equal? says the Holy One" (Isa 40:25).

God is not limited by sexuality, as humans are. Rather, God created sexuality and transcends it. We use metaphors for God to help us understand God. In the case of the metaphor father, it might be helpful to use the term the same way St. Gregory of Nazianzus explained it: The titles "father" and "son" are not descriptors of the essence of God, the gender of God, or the sexuality of God; rather they describe the relationship of two aspects of the Godhead. The Creator is called "the Father" because that is the relationship of the Creator to Christ. Christ is called "the Son" because that is the relationship of Christ to the Creator; the Creator is the source of Christ, and Christ originated by the Creator.[6]

God as Mother

Yet the image of the mother is still important in helping Christians to develop a more full understanding of God. After all, both female and male are made in God's image (Gen 1:27). Since women are made in the image of God, they carry the image of God within them, and therefore their attributes can point us back to God.

Love is one of those attributes, and one of the most profound images of human love is that of a mother and her infant. The story of the two harlots appearing before Solomon in 1 Kings 3:16-28 illustrates the intensity of a mother's love for her child—an intensity that knows no justice, no possessiveness, no selfishness. It is pure, unadulterated love. The one mother would rather lose her child to the other harlot than have her child split in two: "compassion for her son burned within her" (v. 26). The word compassion in Hebrew is the plural noun *rahamim;* in its singular form, *rehem,* the word means "uterus." In Hebrew, words have no vowels, just consonants, and most words stem from a root word consisting of three consonants. The root word for *rahamim* and *rehem* is *rhm,* meaning "uterus." When used as an adjective, the root word *rhm* means "merciful." When used as a verb, it means "to show mercy." A woman's uterus, then, is the physical and concrete basis for the one who shows mercy or is compassionate. Just as the womb warms, nourishes, and protects, and then releases to growth and wholeness, so one who shows mercy and compassion empowers others to grow. Mercy and compassion are feminine traits.[7]

In the Old Testament, Yahweh is repeatedly described with this feminine trait through the word merciful (*rahum*), an adjective that is not ascribed to any creature[8] (see Deut 4:31; 2 Chron 30:9; Neh 9:17; Ps 78:38; 86:16; 103:8; 111:4; 112:4; 145:8; Joel 2:13; Jonah 4:2). The metaphor of God's womb-like compassion is extended in Jeremiah 31:20 (NASB), where Yahweh speaks directly:

> "Is Ephraim my dear son?
> Is he a delightful child?
> Indeed, as often as I have spoken against him,
> I certainly still remember him;
> Therefore my heart yearns for him;
> I will surely have mercy on him," declares the Lord.

The word in line five translated "heart" is *me'ay hamu,* a word used elsewhere for womb (see Gen 25:23; Ps 71:6; Isa 49:1; Ruth 1:11). Interpreting the word as "womb" is substantiated by line six where two verb forms of the Hebrew root word *rhm* are used: *rahem* and *'arahamennu.* With three references to the womb and words related to the womb, this verse provides a powerful feminine metaphor for the womb-like love and mother-like compassion of Yahweh.[9] Old Testament scholar Phyllis Trible translates the last two lines as follows: "Therefore, my womb trembles for him; I will truly show motherly compassion [*rahem 'arahamennu]* upon him. Oracle of Yahweh."[10]

Yet, God's love is even greater than that of a woman for her child. In Isaiah 49, the motherly compassion of God is expressed in verses 10 (*merahamam*) and 13 (*yerahem*). In verse 14, Zion complains that Yahweh has forsaken them. Yahweh responds in verse 15 by explaining that even though a mother might forget her nursing child or else have no compassion (*merahem*) on the child of her womb, God will not forget God's people. Even though it is unthinkable for a woman to forget the child of her womb, it can happen. Yet Yahweh's love is greater than a woman's love for the fruit of her womb, because Yahweh will not forget God's people. While human love has limits, God's love has none. The writer is showing the limits of human metaphors in describing God. Certainly if the womb-love of God were literalized or concretized, we would miss out on the full wonder and extent of God's love.[11]

In the New Testament, Paul uses the metaphor of a pregnant woman carrying a baby to speak of God. According to Clement of Alexandria (Greek theologian, 150–215 C.E.), Paul was paraphrasing a sixth-century-B.C.E. Greek poet named Epimenides in Acts 17:28, when he was preaching to the Athenians: "In him (God) we live and move and have our being."[12]

The child of love in the womb must be born; a pregnant woman must go through labor to give birth. The simile of labor is used to describe the activity of God in Isaiah 42:14b. A simile provides a comparison between two things; one thing is like another. Here, God travails in labor while working to bring forth something new, just as a woman agonizes during labor: "Now I will cry out like a woman in labor (*kayyoleda*), I will gasp and pant."[13]

God also is described as giving birth—a clearly maternal image—to Israel in Deuteronomy 32:18: "You were unmindful of the Rock that bore (*yeladeka*) you; you forgot the God who gave you birth (*meholeleka*)." *Meholeleka* describes only the act of a woman giving birth (see Isa 13:8; 26:17; 51:2; 54:1).[14]

Jesus used the birth image to describe being born of the Spirit. He used the maternal image of being born of God (John 1:13). He expanded the idea by using the image of a mother giving birth as a metaphor for the Spirit giving birth to a new Christian (John 3). When Nicodemus asked Jesus how one could re-enter a mother's womb, Jesus did not change the metaphor; he left the image as a metaphor of a woman giving birth to help Nicodemus understand spiritual birth. 1 John repeats several times the idea that Christians are born of God (3:9; 4:7; 5:1; 5:4; 5:18). Paul also agreed that humans are God's offspring (Acts 17:28-29), trying to give the Greeks' perception of God a more personal angle than that of a graven image.

Moses added to these metaphors in his complaint to God in Numbers 11:12. He implied that God conceived, gave birth, and should therefore be wet nurse for the Israelites. "Did I conceive all this people? Did I give birth to them, that you should say to me, 'Carry them in your bosom, as a nurse carries a sucking child,' to the land that you promised on oath to their ancestors?" Apparently God heard his cry, for God then supplied seventy elders to assist Moses.

The metaphor of a nursing mother is used to describe God's love in Psalm 22:9-10: "Yet it was you who took me from the womb; you kept me safe on my mother's breast. On you I was cast from my birth, and since my mother bore me you have been my God."

To trust upon the breasts of a mother is to be cast upon God from the womb. The writer experienced safety and trust as a child at his mother's breasts, and found the same trust and safety in God as an adult. In addition, God promised to provide the comfort of a mother to those living in Jerusalem: "As a mother comforts her child, so I will comfort you; you shall be comforted in Jerusalem" (Isa 66:13). The comfort and blessings of the breasts are extended to others in Genesis 49:25: "By the God of your father, who will help you, by the Almighty (*sadday*) who will bless you with blessings of heaven above, blessings of the deep that lies beneath, blessings of the breasts (*sadayim*) and of the womb." Notice the play on the words translated "Almighty" and "breasts." *Sadday* literally means "mountains," giving a visual image of the blessings of the breasts. Both words have the root *sdy*.[15]

Jesus even depicted himself as a nursing mother. He said, "Let anyone who is thirsty come to me, and let the one who believes in me drink. As the scripture has said, 'Out of the believer's heart (*koilia*) shall flow rivers of living water' " (John 7:37b-38). According to Bauer's lexicon, *koilia* can refer to the area around the heart—where the breasts are.[16] Christ nurtures seekers at the divine metaphorical breast. The apostle Paul encouraged Christians to nurse at the divine metaphorical breast (remember, at this time in history there was no baby formula; all babies nursed at their mothers' breasts): "Like newborn infants, long for the pure, spiritual milk, so that by it you may grow into salvation—if indeed you have tasted that the Lord is good" (1 Pet 2:2-3).

Feminine images taken from other roles played by humans can help one understand God more fully. For instance, Psalm 123:2 reads, "As the eyes of servants look to the hand of their master, as the eyes of a maid to the hand of her mistress, so our eyes look to the Lord our God, until he has mercy upon us." Here, God is compared to both a master and mistress to whom slaves would look for assistance. This mistress, compared to God, can also be compared to the excellent wife in Proverbs 31. This woman is in charge of an extended household (v. 21), which would probably include servants and slaves. She also provides a feminine role model within the Godhead for women to look to for guidance.

Along with human role models, the animal kingdom provides metaphors of the feminine side of God. In Genesis 1:2 (NIV), one might be reminded of a female bird hovering over her nest: "The Spirit of God was hovering over the waters." The image of another female bird depicts God in Deuteronomy 32:11: "As an eagle stirs up its nest, and hovers over its young; as it spreads its wings, takes them up, and bears them aloft on its pinions." In Hosea 13:8, God's fierce rage is compared to that of a mother bear robbed of her cubs, and to that of a devouring lioness.

God as Sophia

The Old Testament helps humans to understand other feminine aspects of God by personifying the wisdom of God as a woman. The woman is commonly called Sophia because the Greek word for wisdom is *sophia,* a feminine word. The Hebrew word for wisdom, *hokmah,* also is feminine. Wisdom appears, with feminine pronouns, primarily in Proverbs 8:12-31, but also elsewhere. Compare parts of Proverbs 8 with John 1:1-4 and Colossians 1:15-16:

> I, wisdom, live with prudence, and I attain knowledge and discretion. . . . By me kings reign, and rulers decree what is just; by me rulers rule, and nobles, all who govern rightly. . . . The Lord created me at the beginning of his work, the first of his acts of long ago. Ages ago I was set up, at the first, before the beginning of the earth. . . . When he established the heavens, I was there, when he drew a circle on the face of the deep. . . . Then I was beside him, like a master worker; and I was daily his delight, rejoicing before him always. . . . For whoever finds me finds life, and obtains favor from the Lord; but those who miss me injure themselves; all who hate me love death. (Prov 8:12, 15, 16, 22, 23, 27, 30, 35, 36)

> In the beginning was the Word, and the Word was with God, and the Word was God. He was in the beginning with God. All things came into being through him, and without him not one thing came into being. What has come into being in him was life, and the life was the light of all peoples. (John 1:1-4)

> He is the image of the invisible God, the firstborn of all creation; for in him all things in the heaven and on earth were created, things visible and invisible, whether thrones or dominions or rulers or powers—all things have been created through him and for him. (Col 1:15-16)

The parallels in these three passages are striking. Both Wisdom and Christ are begotten by God (the Hebrew word *kanach,* translated "created," also is used of Eve in Genesis 4:1[17]; both are with God in the beginning; both are involved in the work of the creation of the earth; both are involved with humanity; and both give life to humanity. The parallels are even more striking when one considers that Jesus referred to himself as wisdom with a feminine pronoun: "The Son of Man came eating and drinking, and they say, 'Look, a glutton and a drunkard, a friend of tax collectors and sinners!' Yet wisdom is vindicated by her deeds" (Matt 11:19). Paul called Jesus the wisdom of God (1 Cor 1:24), and said in Christ are hidden "all the riches of . . . understanding and . . . knowledge" (Col 2:2-3). The similarities are so striking that theologians in the fourth century C.E. used them to prove the full divinity of Christ during controversies over the nature of Christ.[18]

Another comparison between Sophia and Christ can be made in Proverbs 1:20-23. These verses provide an image of Sophia preaching in the streets, urging listeners to turn from their foolish ways so she can pour out her spirit upon them. It would hardly be considered feminine in ancient Israel to shout and cry out in public places, but this is the image we have of the assertive, feminine side of God preaching truth. Jesus did much the same thing—assertively proclaiming truth in public places (enough to get himself executed) and telling his followers the Spirit would be poured out upon them (Luke 24:49; John 14:16-17).

The sex of Jesus the male who walked the earth is not the totality of who he was, and this needs to be considered in worship of God. Since Christ is identified as feminine wisdom, then we cannot say Christ was male only. Jesus described himself as a mother hen who gathers her chicks under her wings: "How often I wanted to gather your children together, just as a hen gathers her brood under her wings, and you would not have it!" Note the parallels of this image with Psalms 17:8, 36:7, and 91:4. Jesus also described himself as a nursing mother. He used parables about God as a woman, such as the bakerwoman and the woman householder who lost a coin.

In addition, after Jesus was resurrected, he became a "life-giving spirit" (1 Cor 15:45), and his body the church (Acts 9:4), which is described in feminine terms as the bride of Christ. The risen Christ, therefore, is not exclusively male or sexually male.[19] So when women are baptized into the church, they "put on Christ," yet do not become males or take on more masculine characteristics.[20]

Jesus also identified himself with God not as a male, but as a verb of being. Just as God identifies God's self in Exodus 3:14 as I AM, so Jesus identifies himself as the I AM in John 8:58.

For Christians, to ignore the feminine side of God is to ignore a great deal of who God is. To paste feminine characteristics onto a male God does not do justice to God, for the Bible clearly says God is not male. Yet neither is God female, nor is God limited by any roles we place upon God, such as the role of father. God embodies feminine and masculine characteristics, yet transcends them. God is beyond human comprehension, yet human comparisons shed some light and aid in our understanding. We must look beyond the limits of our thinking, our images, and our language. God is our creator, our redeemer, the ground of our being, our friend (John 15:15). God is Spirit (John 4:24), the Holy One (Hos 11:9), the I AM (Exod 3:14).

Questions for Reflection

1. Why has it been okay for many Christians to refer to God using masculine figures, such as father and king, but not feminine figures, such as queen or mother?
2. If the feminine images of God make you feel uncomfortable, why do you think that is?
3. What can be done to help you feel more comfortable with a Savior who refers to himself as a mother hen?
4. How do you feel about God's fierce rage being compared to that of a mother bear robbed of her cubs and to that of a devouring lioness? Was God passive in expressing feminine rage? Is it a sin to be enraged? Do you feel anger or rage about an unjust situation you might be in or might have been in? If so, what did you do with your rage and/or pain?
5. Considering Psalm 123:2, does Proverbs 31 change your image of God if God is compared to a woman running a household? Does thinking of God as a female head of a household provide you with a better role model in God?
6. Do any of these feminine images of God help you feel more in touch with God or loved by God in a new way?
7. Do you see any other similarities among Proverbs 8, John 1:1-4, and Colossians 1:15-16?
8. How do you feel now about being made in the image of God?

Notes

[1]Edmund Colledge, OSA, and James Walsh, SJ, trans., *Julian of Norwich: Showings* (New York: Paulist Press, 1978) 293, 295, 301.

[2]Virginia Ramey Mollenkott, *The Divine Feminine* (New York: The Crossroad Publishing Co., Inc., 1983) 9-10.

[3]Sandra M. Schneiders, *Women and the Word* (Mahwah NJ: Paulist Press, 1986) 28-29.

[4]Gerda Lerner, *The Creation of Patriarchy* (New York: Oxford University Press, 1986) 201.

[5]Carol Delaney, "The Legacy of Abraham," in *Anti-Covenant: Counter-Reading Women's Lives in the Hebrew Bible*, ed. Mieke Bal (Sheffield, England: The Almond Press, Sheffield Academic Press Ltd., 1989) 38.

[6]Schneiders, 3.

[7]Phyllis Trible, *God and the Rhetoric of Sexuality* (Philadelphia: Fortress Press, 1978) 33.

[8]Ibid., 39.

[9]Ibid., 45.

[10]Ibid., 50.

[11]Ibid., 50-51.

[12]Leonard Swidler, *Biblical Affirmations of Woman* (Philadelphia: Westminster Press, 1979) 328.

[13]Trible, 64.

[14]Ibid., 62.

[15]Ibid., 61.

[16]Walter Bauer, *A Greek-English Lexicon of the New Testament and Other Early Christian Literature,* 2d ed. (Chicago: University of Chicago Press, 1979) 437.

[17]Francis Brown, S. R. Driver, and Charles A. Briggs, *A Hebrew and English Lexicon of the Old Testament* (London: Oxford University Press).

[18]Ibid., 260-62.

[19]Schneiders, 54.

[20]Ibid., 54-55.

Chapter 11

Hidden Voices Emerging

"You know that the rulers of the Gentiles lord it over them, and their great ones are tyrants over them. It will not be so among you; but whoever wishes to be great among you must be your servant, and whoever wishes to be first among you must be your slave; just as the Son of Man came not to be served but to serve, and to give his life a ransom for many." (Matt 20:25-28)

—Jesus of Nazareth

Jesus rejected models of leadership based on hierarchies and power structures. He wanted his followers to establish a family of equals consisting of individuals serving each other. This meant women were included on equal terms with men. The early church followed his instructions, including women who served as leaders or presiding officers of house churches, and as apostles, prophets, deacons, theological educators, hard workers, and elders.

In the early centuries following the establishment of the church, numerous women continued to serve in authoritative leadership roles for their congregations. There is evidence for them in letters, wall frescoes, inscriptions, memorials, and epitaphs from that period in history. Among them were:

- two slave women who were ministers and leaders in their church in Bythinia during the early second century1
- Paniskianes, a *presbytera,* or priest, in Egypt during the second or third century[2]; her title indicates she taught, baptized, and consecrated the Eucharistic meal[3]
- a woman who broke bread at a Eucharistic celebration, as depicted on an early third-century fresco in the Greek Chapel of the Priscilla Catacomb in Rome[4]
- a woman in northwest Africa who reportedly celebrated the Eucharist and baptized, drawing many believers, around 235[5]

- a woman *presbytera* who was referred to by Cyprian (bishop of Carthage) during the third century
- Ammion, a third-century woman *presbytera*[6]
- Epiktas, a *presbytera* on the Greek island of Thera during the third or fourth century[7]
- Kyria, a teacher in Egypt during the fourth century
- Kale, a *presbytera* in Sicily during the fourth or fifth century[8]
- Flavia Vitalia in Rome, who held the title *presbytera* around 425
- Leta, *presbytera* in the town of Tropea in Italy during the fifth century[9]
- Saint Brigid of Kildare (452-500), in Ireland, who was consecrated a bishop and preached and held churches in large territories; according to a seventh century writing by an anonymous Irish resident, the First Order of Saints (between 440 and 543) was composed primarily of bishops, and women were said to be among their number, offering further evidence of her ordination[10]

During the ninth and tenth centuries, Bishop Atto of Vercelli (northwest Italy) made it clear that women in the early Church had received the Sacred Orders. This included ordination as *presbyterae,* which involved preaching, directing, and teaching. They also were accepted as leaders of their Christian communities. Women deacons were given the responsibility of baptizing and ministering, especially to other women.[11]

As time marched on, however, hierarchical power and governance slowly replaced the servant model of leadership Jesus provided. In the third century, people involved in governing cities began joining churches. They brought into church structures their expertise at organization and leadership models that were effective with large groups of people. One liturgical prayer recorded in the early third century calls for leaders being ordained to "govern" the church members. Church leaders, who saw the church as the successor to Israel, looked to the Old Testament for leadership models.[12] These models were based on power structures and hierarchies.[13]

When it came to disputes, the Christians wanted problems resolved within their own communities. This desire gave rise to bishops' courts. These courts acquired the same legal status as the Roman municipal courts after Constantine adopted the Christian faith in 306. One writer encouraged Christians to view their bishop as their ruler, even as their king.[14] The model of the church as a discipleship of equals serving each other became a part of the past.

It seems fairly certain that many women were called and ordained into Christian ministry in the early churches. It is significant that for decades most of Christianity supported women in those roles, and some continued to support them even into the sixth century. Women were accepted on the same footing as men, as members of Christ's new family of equals.

This family of equals based on the concept of leadership as service can be revived today, both in the home and in churches. To do so, Scripture must be considered before tradition, even tradition that has lasted almost 2,000 years. To change some of the traditions that do not truly follow the Scriptures, one must start in the home. Since Paul calls on all Christians to submit to each other, this submission must first occur in the home between marriage partners.

Equals at Home

How does a couple create a marriage of equality and mutuality in a broken world torn by sin? It is not easy, and both partners need to be committed to the task. They can decide which spouse has greater gifts and experience in certain areas, and delegate decision making likewise. If one spouse has a concern about what the other is doing, the couple should discuss the concern. Occasionally, this might result in changes and improvements. Yet there are always situations in which couples reach impasses. Here are some steps a couple can take to work toward a mutually acceptable agreement.

(1) Set aside time to pray about the disagreement. Impulsive decision making can lead to greater problems and conflicts. Spend time in relaxed silence, waiting on God for insight, wisdom, and guidance (see Jas 1:5-6). Patiently and persistently seek the Lord's will in the matter (see Matt 7:7-12).

(2) If possible, delay the decision. Sometimes it takes awhile to receive answers to prayers. Also, God might use the extra time to work things out.

(3) Consider whoever is affected most by the decision or has a higher emotional stake in it. Let that person make the decision. For example, if the husband wants more children, but the wife is continually exhausted from taking care of the other children, then the final decision should belong to the wife.

(4) Take a course in or read about conflict resolution. This will provide skills that can be useful in promoting healthy dialogue and negotiating a truce without causing damage to the other person.

(5) Seek to compromise (see Luke 14:31-32 and Acts 6:1-6).

(6) If applicable, discuss any biblical principles related to the issue.

(7) Gather more information to promote healthy dialogue between the two of you. Read books, discuss the situation with others, or attend workshops on the issue.

(8) Remember to be willing to submit to each other out of love (see Phil 2:3-4). For two people who truly love each other, this can be an opportunity to express tenderness and care. Be careful, however, to keep this fair. Make sure one person does not end up doing most of the submitting while the other takes advantage of the situation. In some marriages, the relationship is based not on the principle of love but on the principle of power, such as in cases of verbal, emotional, physical, and sexual abuse. In such situations, the person with the least amount of power needs to be very careful about when, how, or even if to submit to the other's wishes. Seek professional assistance to understand and work through the situation. Justice, mutuality, and equality begin in the home, as do love and submission.

(9) If an impasse still exists, seek the assistance of a third party, an objective person who can provide more insight for the two of you.

Equals in the Church

Mutuality, equality, and justice also are important aspects of the church and need to be emphasized more. Part of this process involves recognizing where power is used to dominate, manipulate, threaten, or control others and realizing this is not the way God's Spirit works. It also involves listening to the voices of those who are seldom, if ever, given the opportunity to speak. For example, the voices of nearly all Christian women have been hidden for centuries, and are only now becoming more recognized. Recognizing women's voices in worship and elsewhere in the church is an important aspect of bringing more mutuality, equality, and justice into the church. There are several ways this can be brought about.

(1) Encourage your church to involve more people, including women, in the leading of worship. If your church and/or denomination does not already do so, it could begin allowing women to preach, serve as deacons and elders, serve communion, serve on committees,

collect the offering, and lead in prayer. At national meetings they should be allowed to do the same, as well as vote. In this way, power and authority become more shared, enabling and empowering others to serve God with their spiritual gifts. The image of God as male and female would also become more apparent in the pulpit, where the eyes of the church members usually focus during worship.

(2) Women should be allowed to teach men, if they are not already doing so.

(3) Encourage your church to use more inclusive language. This is especially true of prayers from the pulpit and the selection of hymns. Perhaps your church could investigate purchasing new hymnals, Bibles, lectionairies, and/or prayer books with inclusive language, and using them in parallel with more traditional materials. Perhaps members of your Sunday School class could write to those supplying Sunday School materials and request that they use more inclusive language and visuals.

(4) Rituals in the churches could be broadened to include creative new ideas from members of the congregation, especially when these could bring new or heightened meaning to worship. Perhaps the careful and discerning use of drama, storytelling, and even dance could deepen members' experience of God in church. As members become more receptive to their own creativity, they could grow closer to understanding the Creator aspect of God. This could lead to greater understanding of others and a greater sense of community among members.

(5) Seek other ways to create more of a sense of community among church members. This could include finding ways for women to speak more about their experiences, and for others to learn to better value those experiences. Women could meet to share their stories of faith and the wisdom that grew out of their experiences, and then celebrate their growth toward greater holiness. Perhaps some of these stories could lead to sermons for women to speak from the pulpit.

Keep in mind as you think about and perhaps discuss these options that for some churches, any of these changes would be considered very radical and unacceptable, especially those with long-standing traditions to the contrary. Yet, Jesus came to break down the barriers and the dividing walls (Phil 2:14). Gentle, nonthreatening dialogue with other members can build bridges of understanding that might eventually lead to changes. Change is usually a process that takes place over time, so patience and understanding will be needed. Wait upon the Lord's wisdom for timing and for the gift of the right words to say.

Keep in mind that the Scriptures are clear that women do have gifts the Holy Spirit can use for the kingdom of God. If women had those gifts in the first few centuries, and their services were used for the spread of the kingdom of God, they can still have those gifts today. When women and churches fail to recognize or use their God-given gifts and talents, the body of Christ is weakened. Surely this is not what Christians want.

The church itself can respond to the message of Christ and the gifts of women by listening to women's voices, distributing power within the church for the sake of justice, accepting women on equal footing with men, and becoming a church where old hierarchies are removed and replaced with what early Christians celebrated in their baptism: "There is no longer Jew or Greek, there is no longer slave or free, there is no longer male and female; for all of you are one in Christ Jesus" (Gal. 3:28). By following the above suggestions and/or others you might think of, the church would soon consist of a family of equals in which leadership truly is service.

Perhaps then, as love, mutuality, equality, and justice are modeled and practiced in the home and in the church, these qualities will naturally tend to spill over into society as a whole. The poor and oppressed in our communities, our country, and throughout the world are crying out for these qualities in leadership. Perhaps you and your church can begin to bring this about in your corner of God's world.

Questions for Reflection

1. How would you envision a family of equals in your church?
2. What sort of personal gifts, skills, and strategies will be needed by members of the church to help bring this about?
3. What is your definition of leadership? How does it fit with Jesus' model?
4. What other ways can you think of to bring about equality in the home between spouses?
5. How do you feel about ordination, and why?

6. Can you think of members in your congregation who could offer their gifts in drama, writing, speech, storytelling, dance, song, or art to help create a more worshipful and enriching church service?
7. In a society filled with very busy people, how can you help your church to develop a greater sense of community among its members?
8. Do you see power structures in your church or home that tend to disempower others? What can you do to encourage change?

Notes

[1]Leonard Swidler, *Biblical Affirmations of Woman* (Philadelphia: Westminster Press, 1979) 313.

[2]Karen Jo Torjesen, *When Women Were Priests* (San Francisco: Harper Collins Publishers, 1993) 19-20.

[3]Cullen Murphy, "Women and the Bible," *The Atlantic Monthly,* August 1993, 60.

[4]Torjesen, 52.

[5]Mary Ann Rossi, "Priesthood, Precedent, and Prejudice: On Recovering the Women Priests of Early Christianity, Containing a Translation from the Italian of 'Notes on the Female Priesthood in Antiquity,' by Giorgio Otranto," *Journal of Feminist Studies in Religion 7,* no. 1 (Spring 1991): 85.

[6]Torjesen, 115.

[7]Ibid., 10.

[8]Ibid., 115.

[9]Rossi, 86-87.

[10]Joan Morris, *Against Nature and God* (London: Mowbrays, 1973) 137-38.

[11]Rossi, 90-92.

[12]Torjeson, 155-57.

[13]Elizabeth M. Tetlow, *Women and Ministry in the New Testament* (New York: Paulist Press, 1980) 140.

[14]Torjeson, 155-57.

Selected Bibliography

Adams, Sheri. *What the Bible Really Says about Women.* Macon GA: Smyth & Helwys Publishing, Inc., 1994.

Bal, Mieke, ed. *Anti-Covenant: Counter-Reading Women's Lives in the Hebrew Bible.* Sheffield, England: The Almond Press, Sheffield Academic Press, Ltd., 1989.

Bilezikian, Gilbert. *Beyond Sex Roles: A Guide for the Study of Female Roles in the Bible.* Grand Rapids: Baker Book House, 1985.

Bloesch, Donald G. *Is the Bible Sexist?* Westchester IL: Crossway Books, 1982.

Boldrey, Richard and Joyce. *Chauvinist or Feminist? Paul's View of Women.* Grand Rapids: Baker Book House, 1976.

Brooten, Bernadette J. *Women Leaders in the Ancient Synagogue.* Chico CA: Scholars Press, 1982.

Brown, Joanne Carlson, and Carole R. Bohn, eds. *Christianity, Patriarchy, and Abuse: A Feminist Critique.* New York: The Pilgrim Press, 1989.

Burtchaell, James. *From Synagogue to Church.* Cambridge: Cambridge University Press, 1992.

Coll, Regina. *Christianity and Feminism in Conversation.* Mystic CT: Twenty-Third Publications, 1994.

Collins, John N. *Diakonia: Reinterpreting the Ancient Sources.* New York: Oxford University Press, 1990.

Couliano, Ioan P. *The Tree of Gnosis.* San Francisco: Harper, 1990.

Danielou S. J., Father Jean. *The Ministry of Women in the Early Church.* London: The Faith Press, 1961.

Dunn, James D. G. Word Biblical Commentary. Vol. 38B, *Romans 9-16.* Dallas: Word Books, 1988.

Edwards, Ruth B. *The Case for Women's Ministry.* Cambridge: University Press, 1989.

Eisler, Riane. *The Chalice and the Blade.* San Francisco: Harper & Row, 1987.

Fewell, Danna Nolan. *Gender, Power, and Promise.* Nashville: Abingdon Press, 1993.

Fiorenza, Elisabeth Schüssler. *In Memory of Her.* New York: The Crossroad Publishing Co., 1983.

__________. *But She Said.* Boston: Beacon Press, 1992.

Goppelt, Leonard. *A Commentary on 1 Peter.* Grand Rapids: Wm. B. Eerdmans Publishing Co., 1993.

Gritz, Sharon Hodgin. *Paul, Women Teachers, and the Mother Goddess at Ephesus.* Lanham MD: University Press of America, 1991.

Gryson, R. *The Ministry of Women in the Early Church.* Collegeville MN: Liturgical Press, St. John's Abbey, 1976.

Gundry, Patricia. *Woman Be Free!* Grand Rapids: Zondervan Publishing House, 1977.

Hayter, Mary. *The New Eve in Christ.* Grand Rapids: Wm. B. Eerdmans Publishing Co., 1987.

Hogarth, David George. *Excavations at Ephesus: The Archaic Artemisia.* London: William Clowes and Sons, Ltd., 1908.

Hopko, Thomas, ed. *Women and the Priesthood.* Crestwood NY: St. Vladimir's Seminary Press, 1983.

Howe, E. Margaret. *Women and Church Leadership.* Grand Rapids: Zondervan Publishing House, 1982.

Jewett, Paul K. *Man as Male and Female.* Grand Rapids: Wm. B. Eerdmans Publishing Co., 1975.

__________. *The Ordination of Women.* Grand Rapids: Wm. B. Eerdmans Publishing Co., 1980.

Keener, Craig S. *Paul, Women, and Wives.* Peabody MA.: Hendrickson Publishers, Inc., 1992.

Korsak, May Phil. *At the Start: Genesis Made New.* New York: Doubleday,1993.

Kraemer, Ross S. *Her Share of the Blessings.* New York: Oxford University Press, 1992.

Kroeger, Catherine Clark. "The Classical Concept of 'Head' as Source," Appendix 3, *in Equal to Serve: Women and Men in the Church and Home.* Gretchen Gaebelein Hull, ed. Old Tappan NJ: F. H. Revell, 1987.

Kroeger, Richard and Catherine Clark Kroeger. "Pandemonium and Silence at Corinth." *The Reformed Journal* (June 1978): 6-7, 42, 68.

__________. *Women Elders . . . Sinners or Servants?* New York: Council on Women and the Church of the United Presbyterian Church in the USA, 1981.

__________. *I Suffer Not a Woman.* Grand Rapids: Baker Book House, 1992.

Lerner, Gerda. *The Creation of Patriarchy.* New York: Oxford University Press, 1986.

Longenecker, Richard N. Word Biblical Commentary. Vol. 41, *Galatians.* Dallas: Word Books, 1990.

Marshall, Molly. "When Keeping Silent No Longer Will Do." *Review and Expositor* 83, no. 1 (Winter 1986).

Meyers, Carol. *Discovering Eve.* New York: Oxford University Press, 1988.

Mickelsen, Berkeley and Alvera. *Women, Authority, & the Bible.* Downers Grove IL: InterVarsity Press, 1986.

Mollenkott, Virginia Ramey *The Divine Feminine.* New York: The Crossroad Publishing Co., 1983.

__________. "A Challenge to Male Interpretation: Women and the Bible," *The Sojourners,* 5:2 February 1976.

Moltmann-Wendel, Elizabeth and Jürgen Moltmann. *Humanity in God.* New York: The Pilgrim Press, 1983.

Morris, Joan. *Against Nature and God.* London: Mowbrays, 1973.

Omanson, Roger L. "The Role of Women in the New Testament Church." *Review and Expositor* 83, no. 1 (Winter 1986).

Pagels, Elaine. *Adam, Eve, and the Serpent.* New York: Random House, 1988.

Pantel, Pauline Schmitt, ed. *A History of Women in the West.* Cambridge MA: The Belknap Press of Harvard University Press, 1992.

Pape, Dorothy R. *In Search of God's Ideal Woman.* Downers Grove IL: InterVarsity Press, 1976.

Pomeroy, Sarah B. *Goddesses, Whores, Wives, and Slaves: Women in Classical Antiquity.* New York: Schocken Books, 1975.

Prohl, Russell C. *Woman in the Church.* Grand Rapids: Wm. B. Eerdmans Publishing Co., 1957.

Ralph, Margaret Nutting. *And God Said What?* Mahwah NJ: Paulist Press, 1986.

Raming, Ida. *The Exclusion of Women from the Priesthood: Divine Law or Sex Discrimination?* Metuchen NJ: The Scarecrow Press, Inc., 1976.

Ranke-Heinemann, Uta. *Eunuchs for the Kingdom of Heaven.* New York: Doubleday, 1990.

Reimer, Ivoni Richter. *Women in the Acts of the Apostles: A Feminist Liberation Perspective.* Minneapolis: Fortress Press, 1995.

Rossi, Mary Ann. "Priesthood, Precedent, and Prejudice: On Recovering the Women Priests of Early Christianity, Containing a Translation from the

Italian of 'Notes on the Female Priesthood in Antiquity,' by Giorgio Otranto." *Journal of Feminist Studies in Religion* 7, no. 1 (Spring 1991): 73-93.

Ruether, Rosemary Radford. *Sexism and God-Talk.* Boston: Beacon Press, 1983.

Russell, Letty M., ed. *Feminist Interpretation of the Bible.* Philadelphia: Westminster Press, 1985.

Sawicki, Marianne. *Seeing the Lord.* Minneapolis: Fortress Press, 1994.

Scalise, Pamela J. "Women in Ministry: Reclaiming Our Old Testament Heritage." *Review and Expositor* 83, no. 1 (Winter 1986).

Scanzoni, Letha, and Nancy Hardesty. *All We're Meant to Be.* Waco: Word Books, 1974.

Schmidt, Alvin J. *Veiled and Silenced: How Culture Shaped Sexist Theology.* Macon GA: Mercer University Press, 1989.

Schneiders, Sandra M. *Women and the Word.* Mahwah NJ: Paulist Press, 1986.

Schottroff, Luise. *Let the Oppressed Go Free: Feminist Perspectives on the New Testament.* Louisville KY: John Knox Press, 1993.

Smylie, James H. "The Woman's Bible and the Spiritual Crisis." In *Modern American Protestantism and Its World.* Vol. 12, *Women and Women's Issues.* Edited by Martin E. Marty. Munich: K. G. Saur, 1993.

Spencer, Aida Besancon. *Beyond the Curse: Women Called to Ministry.* Nashville: Thomas Nelson Publishers, 1985.

Stagg, Evelyn and Frank. *Woman in the World of Jesus.* Philadelphia: Westminster Press, 1978.

Stendahl, Kirster. *The Bible and the Role of Women.* Translated by Emilie T. Sander. Philadelphia: Fortress Press, 1966.

Strachan, Elspeth and Gordon. *Freeing the Feminine.* Dunbar, Scotland: Labarum Publications, Ltd., 1985.

Swidler, Leonard. *Biblical Affirmations of Woman.* Philadelphia: Westminster Press, 1979.

Tamez, Elsa. "The Woman Who Complicated the History of Salvation." *New Eyes for Reading: Biblical and Theological Reflections by Women from the Third World.* Edited by John S. Pobee and Barbel von Wartenberg-Potter. Oak Park IL: Meyer-Stone Books, 1987.

Tetlow, Elizabeth M. *Women and Ministry in the New Testament.* New York: Paulist Press, 1980.

Teubal, Savina J. *Sarah the Priestess.* Athens OH: Swallow Press, 1984.

Torjesen, Karen Jo. *When Women Were Priests.* San Francisco: Harper Collins Publishers, 1993.

Trible, Phyllis. *God and the Rhetoric of Sexuality.* Philadelphia: Fortress Press, 1978.

__________. *Texts of Terror.* Philadelphia: Fortress Press, 1984.

Usami, Koshi. *Somatic Comprehension of Unity: The Church in Ephesus.* Rome: Biblical Institute Press, 1983.

Wahlberg, Rachel Conrad. *Jesus According to a Woman.* New York: Paulist Press, 1975.

__________. *Jesus and the Freed Woman.* New York: Paulist Press, 1978.

White, Andrew Dickson. *A History of the Warfare of Science with Theology* 2. New York: D. Appleton and Co., 1925.

Witherington, Ben III. *Women in the Earliest Churches.* Cambridge: Cambridge University Press, 1988.

Zerbst, Fritz. *The Office of Woman in the Church.* Translated by Albert G. Merkens. St. Louis: Concordia Publishing House, 1955.